Contents

Introduction

Independent living skills covers a wide range of skills necessary to cope every day. These include skills such as self-care including dressing, toileting, eating and drinking. In order for these to be learnt the young person needs to be motivated and see the relevance of learning and undertaking these skills in their daily lives. They also need to be at a stage in their development when they could learn these skills. Start too early and your child will not be ready to achieve them and both you and your child may feel disappointed if success is not achieved. When looking through the ideas to help, select one or two which you feel are achievable so that you and your child can see initial success which can then be built upon.

Development of Skills

New skills take regular practice to learn and become automatic. Different young people will need different lengths of time to do this. Persistence, encouragement and praise are essential, remarking on any achievements however small. If a child is not developmentally ready to learn a skill, it may need to be put on hold and tried again at a later date.

Young people develop at their own pace. For example, some young people acquire skills steadily (child 2), while others develop their skills very quickly, then plateau (child 3) and others may be slower to begin with but then catch up (child 1).

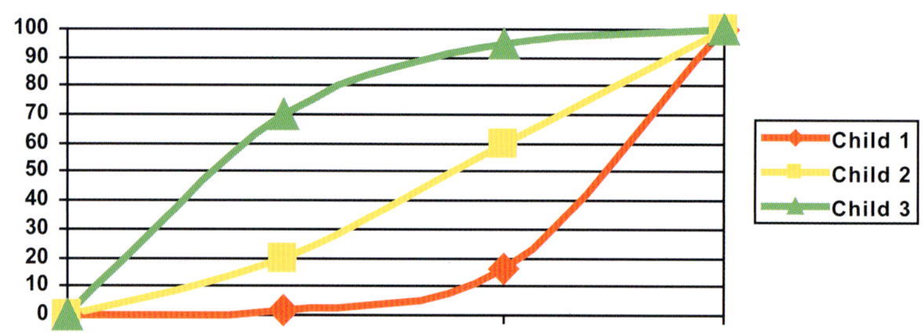

Even though they have taken different paths, many young people reach a functional level if given enough time and practice. Specific age ranges for skill development should be noted with some caution. Some young people may need to spend more time practising and consolidating their skills before moving onto the next stage.

Approximate age of skill development

Feeding

Children begin to finger feed from about 6-12 months old. Beginning to use a spoon and fork usually occurs from about 2-3 years old. Children will generally learn to use a knife to cut soft foods or butter bread from 3-5 years old, and using knife and fork together develops around 4-6 years old.

Dressing

Children often learn to undress before they can dress themselves. From around 2 years old children can assist with dressing by lifting their arms up to take off a t-shirt or pushing their legs through trousers. Between 3–4 years children can put on t-shirts and trousers with elastic waists with some assistance. By 4 years, children are becoming aware of putting clothing on the right way around. 5 year olds should be able to dress with supervision except for some small fastenings. Children can learn to tie shoelaces anywhere from 5-8 years old and some children will need more practice to learn this skill. Tying a neck tie correctly may not be consistent until the child is 10 years old.

Cleaning teeth

Children will help to brush their own teeth from an early age. However they will need to be supervised and a parent or guardian may have to re-brush their child's teeth until they are around 7 years old.

Why Are Mealtimes So Important?

In order to be able to eat independently and enjoy mealtimes, the environment needs to be right. Your child needs to have the foundation skills such as being able to sit in a stable position at the table and be able to use cutlery appropriately.

Disruptive mealtimes can cause arguments and stress amongst the family. Some of the ideas will work for you, but it does depend on the general rules you apply in your household. If everyone is watching television while eating, one child cannot be expected to change his or her habits on their own. Each household will have different rules for mealtimes. There is no right and wrong. However, consistency helps the child considerably. Young people need to learn the rules of mealtimes as they will need these in order to be able to cope in a variety of social situations such as going to friends for tea, lunchtimes in school and special occasions with grandparents.

Young people need to concentrate on what they are eating to be able to taste their foods. There is evidence that young people eat more high fat food while watching television because they are less aware of what they are eating. Mealtimes are also an opportunity for your family to chat together and have a daily catch up. This provides an ideal opportunity for your child to develop their social skills in a 'safe' environment. For example your child can try out jokes to see if they work and others laugh. In addition this time offers an opportunity to practise and improve their conversation skills.

Eating together - mealtime routines

Sitting together for mealtimes provides a safe environment for your child to practise social skills such as talking about their day and what they are eating.

Ideas to help:

- Try to be realistic about how long your child can sit still (around child's age x 2 = minutes sitting at a table e.g. 5 years x 2 = 10 minutes sitting). Better your child sits well for 10 minutes and is praised for this and then gradually builds up the time they can stay than running around during the whole meal and disrupting this for everyone else as well.
- Allow your child to get up and move around between the main meal and dessert if they become restless.
- Encourage your child to lay the table, or to get out the 'right' amount of cutlery for the number of people eating.

- Call your child to the table only when the food is being served.
- Switch off the television to allow your child to concentrate on mealtimes.
- Try to involve your child in the conversation or they may lose concentration. Ideas for example could be to have a family quiz asking each child to tell a good joke, or discussing their favourite programme they have seen on the TV, or film, or a computer game they are playing.

Mealtimes – Where To Start

This section explains the different aspects of mealtime skills in more detail and presents ideas about how to teach the skills successfully.

A good sitting position

Allows the child...

- To be stable, so that arms are free to use cutlery.
- To be comfortable and so remain at the table for longer.
- To be able to concentrate on eating (rather than concentrating on balancing on the chair).
- Opportunities to practise social interactions in a 'safe' environment.

Ideas to help:

- If your child's feet are not able to reach the floor, then place a box or telephone book under their feet so that he or she can sit in a stable position.

Recommended seating position

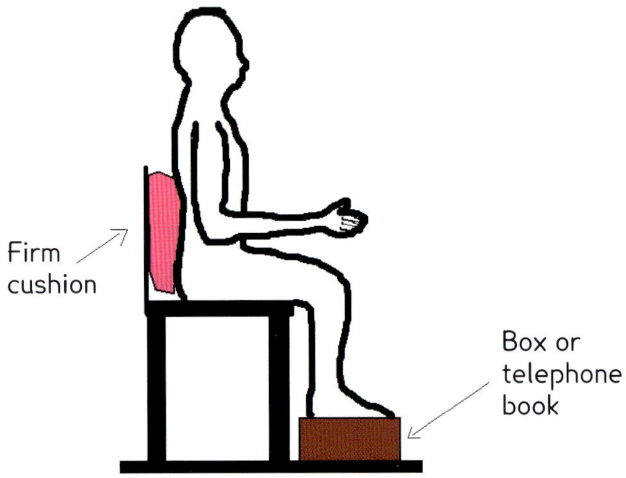

- If the height of the table is too high, place your child on a booster seat or firm cushion or use an adjustable height chair e.g. Tripp Trapp Chair® (available from www.backinaction.co.uk or www.lullabys.co.uk).
- Check your child's back is supported by the back of the chair. Use a firm cushion behind their back if they are too far away.
- If your child finds it difficult sitting at the table for any length of time, bring him or her to the table only when everything is ready so that he or she doesn't have to wait too long to eat, lose concentration and become fidgety.

Equipment - cutlery

By using cutlery appropriately your child is able to:

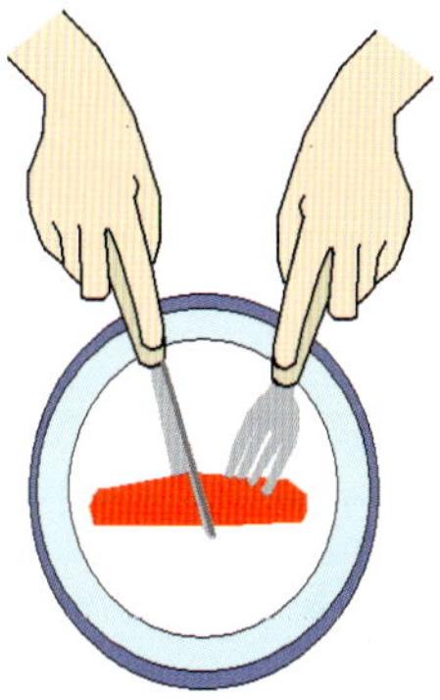

- Eat without help from others.
- Join in socially with the conversation at the table.
- Have a positive effect in school, also potentially improving pencil control.

Ideas to help:

- Make sure cutlery is the right size for your child's hands i.e. you may need to use smaller cutlery before moving to adult-sized cutlery.
- Cutlery with thicker handles or with foam handles may be easier to hold.
- 'Caring Cutlery®' is a specific brand of cutlery which has moulded handles with places to put fingers. This makes it easier for your child to know how to hold the cutlery so that stabbing and cutting the food is more successful. This cutlery can be purchased from mobility shops or similar cutlery can be purchased from Ikea®, or Boots®.

- Try placing an elastic band around the end of the cutlery to prevent the fingers from sliding down when cutting.

Equipment - plates

A plate or bowl that is stable and allows your child to use a knife and fork without food spilling. It also allows the young person to be able to apply extra pressure without the plate moving around the table.

Ideas to help:

- Place a non-slip mat (such as Dycem®) or damp face cloth or tea towel under your child's plate to stop the plate moving on the table.

- Use a soup bowl, deep pasta bowl or a plate with a rim to prevent food spilling over the edge.
- Don't overfill the bowl or plate.

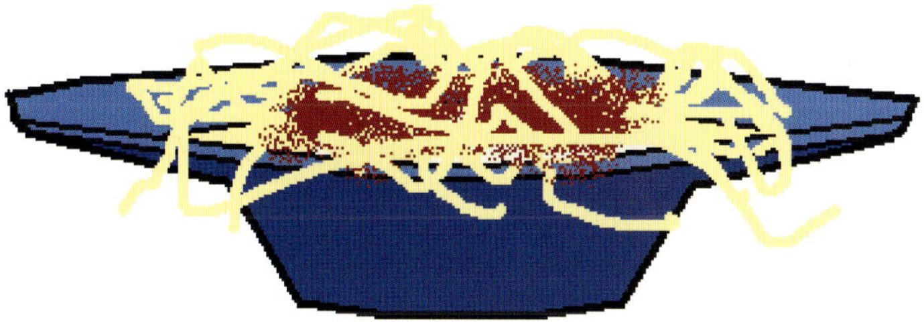

- Place the bowl or plate centred in front of your child and not too far away from him/her.

Equipment - cups

If your child is prone to spilling or tipping their drink try using a cup that is stable and is harder to tip over as this will encourage your child to drink independently.

Ideas to help:

- Try using a two-handled cup as this provides a better grip.
- Try using a weighted or slightly heavier cup – this is less likely to spill.

- If your child still has difficulties drinking from the cup, try using a cup with a lid or straw, or a sports bottle.
- Do not overfill the cup.

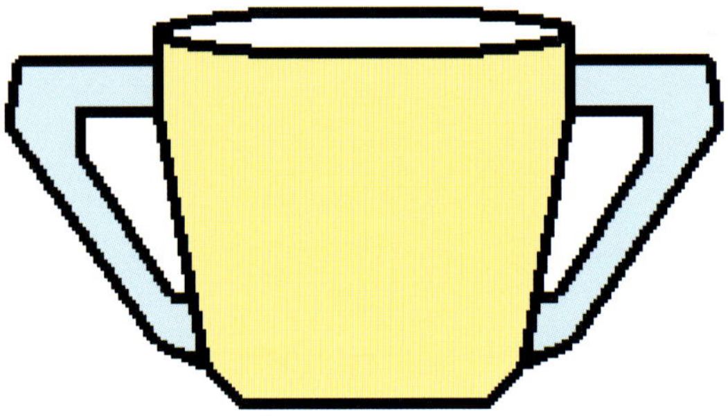

Developing Cutlery Skills

A knife and fork requires your right and left hand to work independently but work co-operatively. This is similar to writing – where one hand stabilises the paper while the other controls the pen.

Ideas to help:

- There are three stages in using cutlery. First, start with a spoon, and then move onto using the fork and getting your child used to sticking this into a variety of firm but soft foods such as carrots and sausages.

- When your child is competent, then introduce a knife alongside the fork. Again, start with foods that are not too difficult to cut up.

- If cutting round food such as potatoes, try slicing the bottom off it to stop it rolling around the plate.
- Try making pretend food using playdough or plasticine and get your child to roll the playdough into a sausage shape, and place on a plate and practise cutting it up.

Playdough recipe – make the playdough into pretend food and use for practising cutlery skills. Your child could be involved in making the playdough as this will also develop their hand skills.

Playdough Recipe

- 1 cup flour
- 1 cup warm water
- 2 teaspoons cream of tartar
- 1 teaspoon oil
- ¼ cup salt
- Food colouring

Mix all the ingredients, adding the food colouring last. Stir over a medium heat until smooth. Remove from the pan and knead until well blended. When cooled place in a plastic bag or airtight container.

Selective eating habits

Some young people may be seen as "fussy" and selective in what they choose to eat, only liking specific food groups such as potatoes and chicken or only crisps and chocolate.

If you are concerned with your child's diet, see your family doctor to check his or her general health, growth and development.

Why may your child have a selective diet?

- Only being introduced to a narrow range of tastes and textures. This may be the case if, for example, you like limited tastes and food groups.
- Your child may dislike some textures of food such as meat. This can be apparent often from an early stage (this may also be linked with language difficulties) and the child may prefer a more "sloppy" diet.
- Food may be used as a way to assert control over family members, or to gain attention.

This can become a battleground when the child refuses to eat. And each mealtime is considered a challenge for both child and parents.

Ideas to help:

- Make mealtimes a pleasant experience for the whole family and not a focus to discuss food issues, especially if this is more focussed on one member of the family. Try to get all family members to avoid this topic of conversation.
- By eating with your child you can show them how you enjoy eating and spending quality time with them.
- Offer your child a smaller portion of the same food you are eating.
- If they do not eat their food, don't make a fuss, just take it away. Try not to give any snacks, sweets, crisps or fizzy drinks between meals. It is harder for your child to refuse to eat if he or she is hungry and young children can feel full after drinking a fizzy drink.
- Encourage your child to try a range of different foods - these should be different colours, textures and tastes . A small amount is fine at first. One way to introduce new tastes is to mix them in with existing foods they like.

- Try "hiding" vegetables in pureed soups, mixed in a cheese sauce, or as a topping on a pizza.
- Use a sauce your child likes with the new food such as introducing fish with tomato sauce, if your child likes this already.
- Try not having crisps, sweets or fizzy drinks in the house at all, if this is all your child will eat. He or she is likely to want them if they are available.
- If your child is thirsty before a meal give a drink of water rather than milk-based drinks as this may fill your child up.
- Praise your child when he or she tries new foods even if he or she decides then they don't like them.
- Involve your child in food preparation so he or she can get interested in how dishes are made and take pride in preparing them and gaining praise from others.

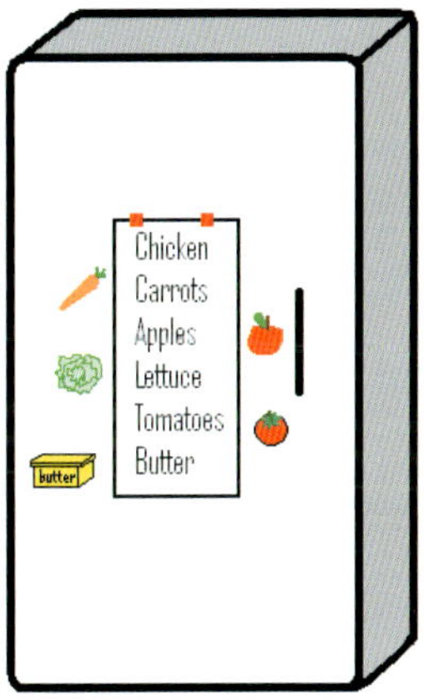

- Introduce raw vegetables and get your child to dip them into a dip they have made, such as mayonnaise with tomato sauce mixed in.
- Find out if there is a local children's cookery course in your area. Your child can see other children trying different foods and this may act as encouragement to try also.

Food texture

Check to see if your child eats a variety of different textured foods:

Does your child eat at least one food from each of these categories every day?

Soft foods e.g.	**Crunchy foods e.g.**	**Lumpy foods e.g.**
Fromage Frais	Cereal	Yoghurt with fruit bits
Cooked carrots or potatoes	Toast	Apple pie with custard
Soup	Dry biscuits	Mashed potatoes
Sandwiches	Crisps	Mince with vegetables in it

If **YES**, then it is unlikely that their selective eating is related to texture.

If **NO**, then the food preferences could be related to the texture of the food.

Ideas to help if your child has texture-related difficulties:

- Respect that your child has a genuine problem with putting certain textures of food in their mouth. Specific textures can cause some young people to "gag" or be physically sick.
- Offer one new food texture at a time with other familiar foods e.g. adding a few peas into mashed potatoes.
- Encourage your child to try new tastes and give lots of praise for effort if they do; but don't force your child.
- Eat with your child so they can see you eating a variety of foods.
- Don't make too much of a fuss if your child won't eat a certain food; take it away and re-offer similar foods again a few weeks later.

School mealtimes

School mealtimes can feel a stressful time for some young people. Not knowing what to do and where to go can feel very confusing. If there are additional difficulties about what to choose to eat this can make the child very anxious.

Young people may have difficulties around mealtimes for a variety of reasons:

- Knowing where to queue to get food, especially where there may be more than one choice such as hot foods or a salad bar.
- Choosing which food they want, especially if they are anxious and are slow in making a decision when there are others queuing behind them.
- Knowing where to sit and who to sit next to can cause anxiety. Making a wrong decision can have major consequences, if they are not aware of the unwritten social etiquette in the school (such as juniors don't usually sit next to infants).

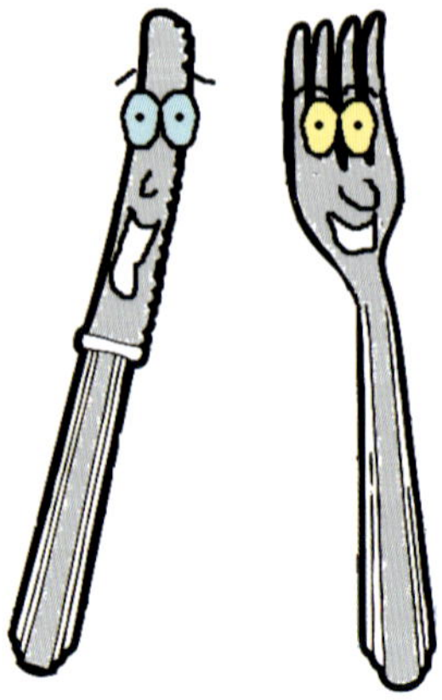

- Balancing and walking with a full tray of food with a drink.
- Using a knife and fork.
- Managing packed lunches such as opening the lunchbox, opening a crisp packet or inserting a straw into a drink.
- In a secondary school setting, handling money and getting the right change may cause difficulties if the child is slower than their peers, especially if there are others waiting behind them.

Ideas to help:

- Check what the routine is for lunch and what choices (if any) there are. How are lunches paid for?
- Ask if the menu can be sent home so you can discuss with your child their food choices for the following day.
- Ask the teacher if there is a buddy system if your child is anxious knowing who to sit by. This will reassure your child so that he or she knows who they will sit next to. This could be an older child to start with who they can follow until they know the routine.

- If your child has difficulty carrying a tray, try to suggest to the SENCO or class teacher that your child could place a piece of non-slip matting on the tray to prevent the plate moving. This may be useful for all students so that difficulties one child has are not highlighted to peers.
- If your child spills something on his or her clothes regularly, suggest to them that they remove their jumper before eating so they have something clean to put back on after lunch.
- Practise opening containers, crisp packets, and putting straws in cartons at home if this is difficult. Alternatively pre-open packets and give a drink in a sports bottle with a spout.

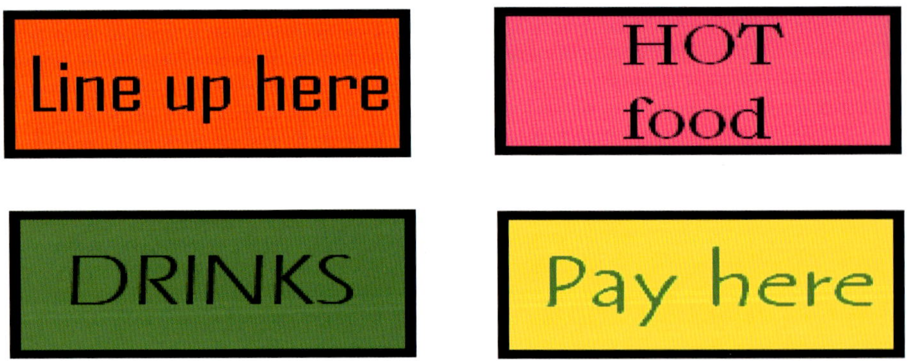

Bath Time – Where To Start

Bath time can be fun or can be a cause for family arguments. This can start with not getting in, not wanting to be washed or wash themselves, or disliking having their hair washed.

Ideas to help:

- Make bath time interesting – put some clean yoghurt cartons or pouring jugs in the bath, use soap/bath crayons or shaving foam to draw mystery notes. Try not to show your child you are in a hurry. Talk through the day or tell a story to your child.
- If your child has difficulties with balance they may find sitting in a slippery bath being washed a scary experience. Try using a non-slip mat for getting in and out of the bath.

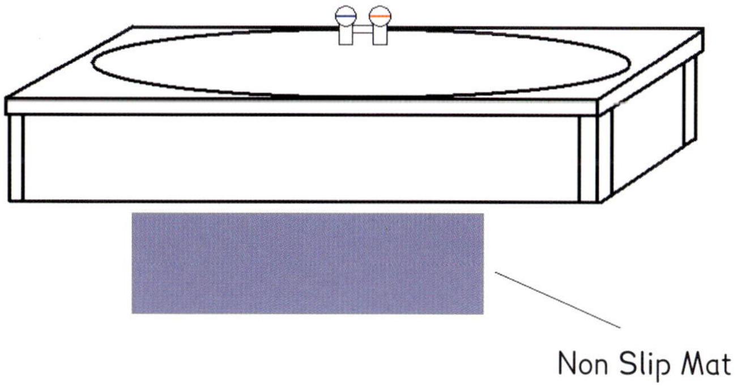

- If your child likes specific TV or cartoon characters they often make shampoo bottles with the characters on them. This may encourage your child into the bath.
- If your child has no concept of time in the bath, then use a timer so that he or she can see or hear when time is up and they need to get out.
- If your child hates having his or her hair shampooed you could use a shampoo guard so that your child can sit upright with their eyes open. Mothercare® sell a "shampoo shield", and there is also a Clippasafe®, Shampoo Eye Shield® sold for the same purpose. Both are similar foam rims which sit on the child's head so water does not go into your child's eyes.
- If your child is fearful of getting soap in his or her eyes, there are several makes of shampoo that claim to be better for this such as Johnson's "No More Tears Baby Shampoo®" and Paul Mitchell's "Baby Don't Cry Shampoo®".
- Ask your child to help wash his or her own hair.

Hair cutting

Some children do not like the sensation of having their hair cut, or they find it hard to sit still for any length of time.

Ideas to help:

If your child does not like to have his or her hair cut you could try:

- Taking him or her to hairdressers who are used to cutting children's hair where there are other children around and the hairdresser will be patient if your child is fidgety.
- Let your child take a hand-held toy or computer so they can play with this while their hair is being cut.
- Plan an activity after hair cutting to motivate your child to sit still for a short time.
- If your child does not like having his or her hair touched try gently but firmly massaging their head so that your child gradually gets used to having their head touched.

- Some hairdressers will come to your home so that your child is in a familiar environment when they are having their hair cut.
- Only bring your child to the chair when everything else is ready. Don't make them wait as they could become more anxious.

Nail cutting

Some children can't stand the sensation of having their nails cut. Getting your child to sit still for long enough may become a battle between you.

If your child does not like to have his or her nails cut you could try:

Ideas to help:

- Try cutting your child's toenails after a bath when they are softer and your child is more likely to be more relaxed.

- Distract your child by getting them to watch TV or a video while it is being done. Have someone else with you who can talk/act as a distraction.
- Alternatively consider cutting your child's nails while he or she is sleeping if it is a real battle every time.
- Nail clippers or manicure scissors designed for infants are best. The tips are rounded for safety.
- Offer a reward to your child if they manage to sit still while you are cutting.

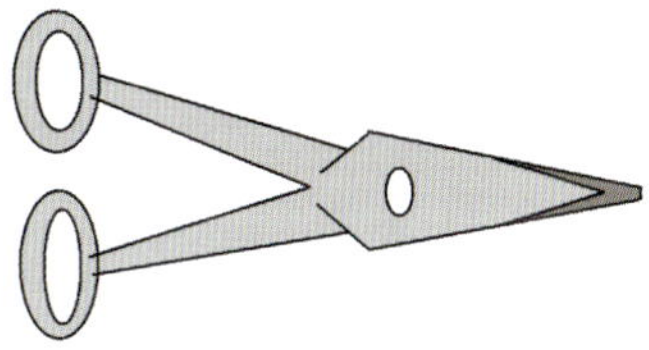

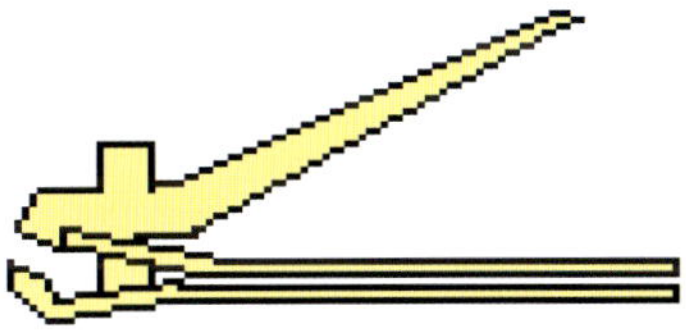

Using the toilet

Some young people especially with co-ordination difficulties find the task of wiping their bottom difficult. This may be because they do not have the balance to take their hand behind them to wipe, forget the sequence of the steps in the task or do not have the co-ordination to do the wiping action with accuracy. This is acceptable in a younger child but as the child grows older it can be a source of family conflict resulting in the child being embarrassed by stained pants (and sometimes hiding them from parents) or avoiding going to the toilet and becoming constipated. This may lead to a further set of difficulties with tummy pain and a fear of going to the toilet with the child worrying even more.

Ideas to help:

- If the toilet is adult size, your child may prefer a child's toilet insert, so he or she feels more stable when sitting. Mothercare® sell a "2-in-1 Toilet trainer seat" which has an inner seat as well as a traditional sized seat.

- Support your child's feet by placing a box or step under them. Then when they bring themselves forward to wipe, their balance is maintained.
- Your child could also support themselves by holding onto the basin or a fixed rail, if these are close to the toilet and it is safe to do so.
- Try using wet-wipes instead of toilet paper, as these can help with cleansing and are often easier to wipe. Some of these are now specifically marketed for young people.
- Give your child a small packet of wet-wipes to go to school.
- Teach your child to wipe 5 times and check, as they may not be able to feel when they are clean so it may help to have a specific number of times to wipe.
- Practise the movement needed for bottom wiping. For example passing a ball or balloon around the body when standing or sitting; or playing tunnel ball where a ball is rolled between the legs. In the bath play games such as putting shaving foam "blobs" at different places on your child's back for them to wipe off.
- If your child cannot remember the sequence of actions to be done, provide a visual reminder of these for him or her to follow.

Pictures for this can be downloaded free from www.dotolearn.com. A number of pictures are also included in this pack.

- Encourage your child to go to the toilet regularly after meals to encourage a regular bowel habit.
- If your child has soiled his/her pants and he or she is older, encourage putting the soiled pants in the washing machine and washing them. Try to praise effort even if he or she is still making some mistakes.

Teeth cleaning

Some young people don't like the sensation of placing a toothbrush inside their mouths and cleaning their teeth.

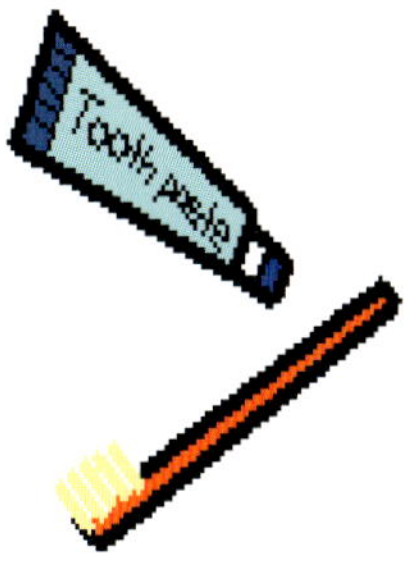

Ideas to help:

- Try using an electric toothbrush along with a timer so that your child knows how long to brush his/her teeth.
- An electric toothbrush also offers a more consistent brushing pattern and it is more likely to clean your child's teeth more effectively than an ordinary toothbrush.
- If your child has a favourite TV character, products such as toothbrushes and toothpaste are available with different characters, which could add interest and motivation. Further information, activities for young people and products are available from http://www.dentalhealth.org.uk
- Try using a children's mouthwash to help with their oral hygiene. Gargling, swishing and spitting out the mouthwash can be fun for children to do.

- Your child may be more comfortable sitting on a chair or stool to brush their teeth.
- Use rewards such as a star chart to encourage your child to brush twice a day.
- It is recommended that you continue to supervise and brush your child's teeth until they are at least 7 years old. For some children it may be for longer.

Using a Star Chart

A star chart is one method that can be used as a visual reward system. For it to work successfully you will need to explain to the child exactly how it is going to be used. Clear and simple rules need to be agreed and then applied consistently and fairly. Discuss what reward your child would like to aim for, and negotiate this together. This approach is often useful to motivate your child to change habits but they may become bored if the same targets are set for more than a few weeks. Think about reviewing it and changing the targets as they are achieved so that your child remains interested and motivated.

Set both short and longer-term rewards. A short-term reward may be one set for the day and mean the child, for example, can stay up an extra 10 minutes. A longer-term goal, for example, could be to collect 12 stars in one week. If they achieve this then an additional reward could be given such as playing a game together or going on an outing. Make sure all targets are potentially achievable in the time frame.

Stars could be given, for example, for cleaning their teeth, for putting clothes in drawers, putting dirty washing in the laundry, going to bed on time.

As an example a star chart could look like this:

my star chart	Total
Monday	2
Tuesday	3
Wednesday	1
Thursday	3
Friday	4
Saturday	2
Sunday	2

Dressing

Being able to dress requires a number of different skills. Once achieved, this allows your child increased independence. It requires a number of skills including being able to balance, have good fine motor co-ordination (needed for doing buttons and zips) and being able to plan and correctly sequence the order in which the clothes are put on and orientate them in the right way. If dressing and undressing are difficult then it may result in your child being slower to get to PE in school or out to play, and slower getting down for breakfast in the morning.

Ideas to help:

- Try getting your child to dress themselves whilst sitting down, so they are more stable.
- Help your child to put their clothes on the right way by pointing out logos on their clothes and telling them that they always go at the front or that labels at the top of the garment are always at the back.
- Encourage your child to lay out their clothes in the evening in the order they need to put them on. Try to keep this routine the same, such as pants first, then socks, then T-shirt etc.

- Practise buttoning with large buttons and holes, perhaps on another family member's clothes. Practise when you are both not in a rush.
- Button shirts from the bottom up so the buttons and holes can be lined up correctly and your child can see what he or she is doing.
- Buttons sewn on with shearing elastic allow the button to be pulled further away from the fabric. This is very useful for cuffs where these are harder to do and undo.
- If fastening buttons is very difficult, try sewing up the button holes and sewing the buttons onto the closed holes so it looks like they are done up. Sew a small piece of Velcro onto the back of each button so the shirt can just be pressed together. You may like to just use this technique for the top collar button, as this can be the most difficult, since your child may not be able to see what they are doing.
- Attach a small piece of string/ribbon or small toy to the eye of a zip to make it easier to pull.
- Poppers on clothes are also an alternative fastening.
- Choose tops with V necks so your child can easily see which way around they go.
- Elasticated trousers are easier to pull on and off than ones with a fastening at the top for younger children.

- If dressing is a real problem for PE days in school, consider wearing PE kit under the school uniform.
- If tying a tie is difficult then use a tie on elastic, or alternatively make up the tie as it should look, cut the loop at the back and sew Velcro to each cut side. This means the tie looks right but is easy to put on and off.
- Try teaching your child to tie a tie by standing behind them when you are guiding them rather than standing opposite them - place your hand over theirs. Good websites with pictures of how to do it are: http://www.tieguide.com/four-in-hand.htm or at http://www.tieanecktie.com/WindsorKnot.php.

Shoelaces

Some young people may take longer to learn to tie their shoelaces. If your child is not ready to tie their laces, try to get shoes with Velcro until they are a bit older. Some young people may never master the art of tying their laces and for these young people there are alternative laces available (elastic and spring laces). Many adults get through life without laces in their shoes. It is no longer an essential skill for life.

Ideas to help:

When teaching your child to tie their shoelace, try:

- Sitting on the floor with your child's back against a wall so they are in a stable position or alternatively on a low chair.
- Try tying different colour laces together such as one red and one yellow and thread these through a trainer to teach. Talking through as well as showing will help your child. "Place the yellow lace over the red one and pull..." etc.)

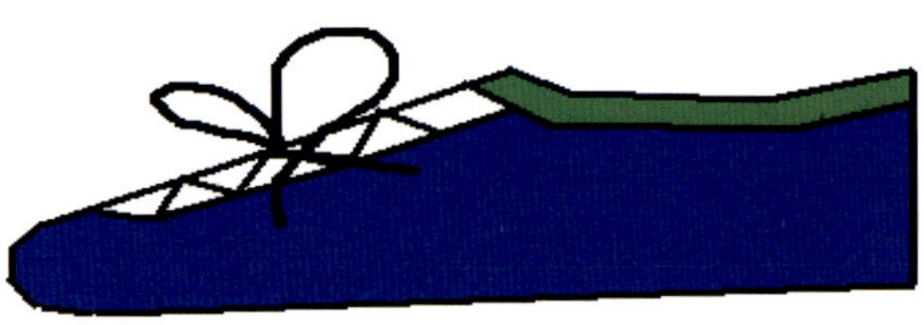

- Different colour laces make it easier for the child to see what he or she is doing.
- A double knot is less likely to slip open. To do this place one lace across the shoe and the other lace crossing over it. Tuck the top lace through the loop twice and then pull on both ends of the laces to tighten. By passing the lace through twice it secures the knot so that your child can let go of the laces without it becoming loose. You could say to your child "Over and under and pull, over and under and pull". Keep instructions as simple as you can.
- Once you have done this then try making two loops such as the 'bunny loops method'. This means that you need to make two loops with each lace and then pass one loop over the other one and pull through. This means the instructions can again say "Over and under and pull" once the loops have been made.
- A useful site is Ian's shoe lace site http://www.fieggen.com/shoelace/knots.htm. This site shows a number of ways of tying laces including the bunny loop method. Another site which demonstrates how to tie laces through a short video is http://www.videojug.com/film/how-to-tie-your-shoelaces

- Elastic shoelaces are available, so your child can pull his or her shoes on and off without having to undo the lace. These are available from mobility shops. 'Lock laces®' are elastic laces with a special spring lock on them. This means that they do not need to be tied up and they remain secure. They are also available in a variety of colours and can fit many trainers. Details of stockists can be found at http://www.1000mile.co.uk/locklaces.htm.

Bedtime and sleep

Young people can have difficulties getting off to sleep or staying asleep all night for a variety of reasons such as a change of environment (new house), worry about a change in their lives (new school), or not acquiring good sleeping habits.

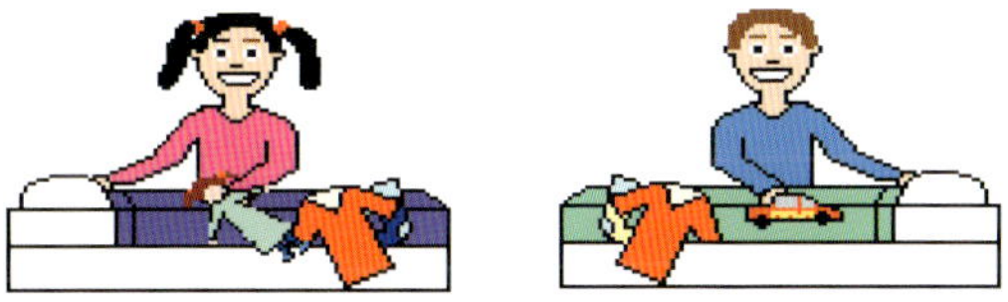

Ideas to help – the bedroom environment:

Creating a calm and comfortable bedroom will help your child settle down for sleep. Consider the following for your child's bedroom:

- Is there too much or too little light? Try a night light if your child does not like the dark. If the room is too bright try heavier curtains or blackout linings for the curtains. A blanket over the window would also work.
- Is the room too hot or too cold? Children do not sleep as well in an over-heated room. Try leaving a window open to allow fresh air to circulate.

- What is the noise level like? Can your child still hear the television or conversations? You may want to play some quiet music so your child can listen to this or let your child listen to a story on a tape till he or she drifts off to sleep.
- Is your child's bed comfortable? If the bed is over ten years old it may not be comfortable and may need changing.
- Is the bed placed by the door or by a draught - could the position of the bed be changed?
- Does your child have asthma or any allergies to dust mites? These are present in all mattresses and may cause your child to cough or sneeze through the night. Make sure you vacuum the bed regularly. You can also get a mattress cover that can be washed that can reduce dust mites, available from most major stores.
- Is your child's bedroom too stimulating for them? Are there too many posters on the walls; can they see all their games and toys; do they have a TV or computer in their room? If possible try to put toys and books away on a shelf (which can then be covered by a curtain) or in a box or drawer.
- Does your child feel safe in their bed? Your child may prefer to have a low bed or mattress on the floor.

Also, consider placing a soft blanket on the floor so if they do fall out they are less likely to hurt themselves. A tightly rolled up blanket placed on the edge of the bed under the bottom sheet to prevent them from accidentally rolling out of bed may also add to your child's feeling of security. Placing your child in a sleeping bag instead of a duvet can have a similar effect.

- Try using blankets. Some children prefer the "weight" of a blanket and they can also be tucked in. Place the bed against the wall.
- Does your child sleep with the door open or closed? Do they have any fears about being in their room on their own? It is quite common for young people to have fears about going to bed. Try talking to your child about their fears. Ask them what they are afraid of and respect what they say. Reassure and support your child about how real these fears are. It is not helpful to ignore your child's fears or put them down by saying things like 'you are being a baby for being afraid of that'. Try not to over-react as your child will pick up on your emotions. More information on young sleep problems in childhood and adolescence can be found at: http://www.rcpsych.ac.uk/mentalhealthinformation/mentalhealthandgrowingup/7sleepproblemsinchildhood.aspx

Ideas to help – the bedtime routine:

- Try using the same routine each evening, such as teatime, a warm bath, story and then bed. This prepares your child for sleep.
- Increase physical activity late afternoon so your child is physically tired.
- Bedtime should be about the same time every night.
- Your child may need a favourite toy to take to bed with them.
- Your child may need time to settle and should be allowed to read or listen to quiet music in bed until he or she feels drowsy.
- A massage with baby oil, perhaps with some lavender oil drops in it, may help relax your child before bed. Try to massage firmly as light, 'tickly' massages may over-stimulate some young people.
- Try to encourage your child not to eat too much close to bedtime. Avoid drinks containing caffeine such as tea, coffee or cola or fizzy drinks, if you can.
- Try to avoid loud and exciting TV programmes or computer games just before bedtime. It may take an hour or two to calm down after playing an exciting game.

- Has your child any worries over school or with friends that he or she needs to discuss before bed? Create an opportunity to talk during the evening such as at teatime, on the way home from school, bath time or before bedtime. Decide with your child the best time to do this.
- If your child gets up and comes in to you every night, take them back to bed and reassure them you are close by. Minimise the fuss and avoid giving them too much attention by talking to them. You will need to be consistent and you may need to do this a dozen times the first night! Be persistent and your child will realise that they need to sleep in their own bed and you are close by.

Useful Pictures for a Dressing schedule

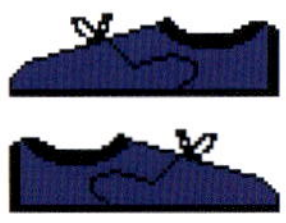

Put school shoes on

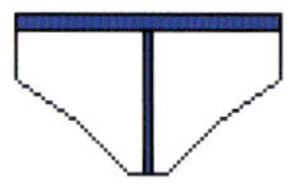

Put on underwear

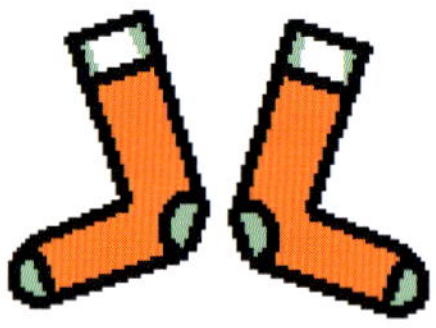

Put on socks

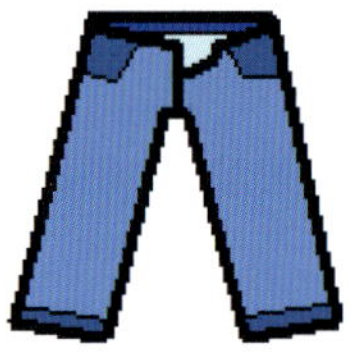

Put on trousers

Put on shirt

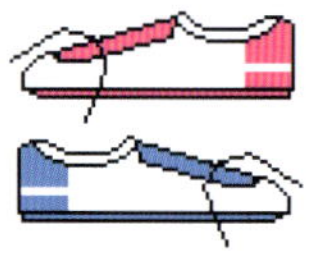

Put trainers on

Put on tie

Put on jumper

Getting dressed

Put on skirt

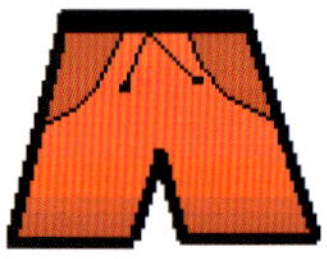

Put on shorts

Put coat on

Useful Resources

Below are a number of websites with further information.

These and others in the pack, along with specific suppliers, are suggestions.

The Dyscovery Centre does not take any responsibility for any items bought from these manufacturers and takes no responsibility for any content on the websites suggested, as the content may change from time to time, beyond our control.

Mealtime Management for Picky Eaters
http://vanderbiltowc.wellsource.com/dh/content.asp?ID=439

5 a day - free downloadable recipes for young people plus games and loads of other information
http://www.5aday.nhs.uk

BBC Food – Cooking with Young People
http://www.bbc.co.uk/food/recipes/mostof_cookingwithyoung_people1.shtml

Vegetarian and Vegan Cooking for Young People and Teenagers
http://www.vegetarian.org.uk/campaignsbadhabits.htm

Back to the Table – Healthy Eating, Family Mealtimes
http://www.raisingkids.co.uk/bttt_2005/home.asp

For Products such as Caring Cutlery and Dycem – Nottingham Rehab Suppliers
http://www.nrs-uk.co.uk/index.html
General Enquiries: 0845 120 4522
(Monday to Friday 8.30am - 5.00pm)

Alternatively you may find useful products at your local mobility aids shop

Mealtime Management for Schools
http://www.schoolsplus.det.wa.edu.au/splus/Services/splus_framework/mealtime_management

Managing Your Child's Weight
http://www.ucsfhealth.org/young_peoples/edu/pedsWeight.html

Shoelace tying site
http://www.fieggen.com/shoelace/knots.htm.

Les auteurs remercient tout particulièrement

**MICHEL DESJOYEAUX, FRANÇOIS GABART,
ARMEL LE CLÉAC'H, VINCENT RIOU,
JEAN LE CAM, JÉRÉMIE BEYOU,
YANN ELIÈS, SAMANTHA DAVIES,
ARNAUD BOISSIÈRES, TANGUY DE LAMOTTE**
et **ROLAND JOURDAIN.**

Pour celles et ceux qui pourraient se retrouver perdus dans les hautes mers
du langage maritime, un petit lexique se trouve en fin de volume.
Vous y trouverez également les auteurs des citations qui jalonnent ce livre.

FRANCE, CÔTE ATLANTIQUE, LES SABLES-D'OLONNE, UNE FOIS TOUS LES QUATRE ANS...
PAR UN FROID PETIT MATIN DE NOVEMBRE, L'EAU DU PORT NE S'EST PAS ENCORE ÉVEILLÉE.

Histoires du
VENDÉE GLOBE

Alexandre Chenet
SCÉNARIO
Renaud Garreta
DESSIN

DARGAUD

LES BATEAUX SONT ENCORE À QUAI MAIS SUR LE PONTON, DÉJÀ, LES ÉQUIPES S'ACTIVENT.
DANS QUELQUES INSTANTS, LE BALLET DES VOILIERS LARGUANT LES AMARRES VA COMMENCER.

LES AMIS, LA FAMILLE, IL EST PASSÉ LE TEMPS DES DISCOURS. UN MOT BALBUTIÉ, DES REGARDS, UNE ÉTREINTE, UNE TRÈS FORTE ÉTREINTE, UN DERNIER AU REVOIR À LA TERRE ET, SELON UNE MINUTIEUSE ORCHESTRATION, LES BATEAUX, UN À UN, S'ÉCARTENT DU BORD.

LES MARINS EMMÈNENT AVEC EUX UN PEU DE NOTRE HUMANITÉ. ILS PARTENT COMME SONT TOUJOURS PARTIS LES HOMMES, VOIR LÀ-BAS, AU-DELÀ.
TOUT AU LONG DU CHENAL, LA FOULE EST PRÉSENTE, JOYEUSE, ADMIRATIVE, FIÈRE.
DANS QUELQUES HEURES, ILS S'ÉLANCERONT, EN COURSE, POUR UN TOUR DU MONDE, SEUL, SANS ESCALE ET SANS ASSISTANCE.

Émotionnellement, le départ c'est chaud. Tu as la mayonnaise qui prend pendant les trois semaines aux Sables-d'Olonne, les skippers, les équipes, les sponsors, les journalistes, le public. C'est une véritable tornade qui monte, qui monte jusqu'au départ.

Être au départ du Vendée Globe, au ponton des Sables-d'Olonne, est déjà une victoire. Tu dois y être amarré trois semaines avant le départ. Pendant ce temps-là, tu ne navigues pas, pas avec ton bateau en tout cas, et chaque jour, tu as des rendez-vous avec les partenaires et les médias. Les équipes majeures – qui n'ont pas eu de gros pépins durant leur préparation, pendant les deux, trois, quatre années précédentes – sont prêtes. Le bateau est chouchouté, le skipper entouré, protégé, son planning est bordé. À l'autre extrémité, tu as les petites équipes qui n'ont pas encore bouclé la préparation du bateau, qui courent à la recherche de tel matériel, de telle info pour le réglage du machin-bidule qui ne sera, de fait, pas testé en conditions. Les rendez-vous médias et partenaires se calent à la petite sauvette et s'empilent jusqu'à l'épuisement, journée après journée. Et entre ces deux opposés, tu as tous les cas de figure, en fonction des budgets, de la relation tissée avec les sponsors, des opportunités, des coups de chance, de malchance et aussi, parce que ça compte énormément, de ta personnalité.

Je me souviens d'être monté à bord d'un bateau, en 2012, à quelques jours du départ… On se serait cru sur le parking de la plage avant une régate de 4.20. "Je peux te prendre ce bout? Il me manque des piles, tu sais si la supérette en vend? On peut faire un test radio pour voir si ça fonctionne?" À la veille d'un tour du monde, c'est chaud quand même.

Je me permets de dire cela parce que ce n'était pas mon premier Vendée Globe, parce que mon bateau était prêt, parce que j'avais trouvé mes sponsors assez tôt durant la préparation. Mais si j'en avais été là où en était ce skipper, pas sûr que j'aurais renoncé au départ. J'aurais certainement fait comme lui et j'y serais allé. C'est le Vendée Globe, une montagne douce, belle et immense… Tu en rêves tellement avant de pouvoir t'y élancer.

Si on met de côté ce qui reste tout de même une exception, on constate alors que le niveau de préparation des équipes va crescendo d'une édition à l'autre. Même les moins aguerries ont une approche de plus en plus professionnelle, consciente et lucide.

Je pense que le fait majeur de ces semaines à attendre le départ, pour nous skippers et skippeuses, c'est le repos. Les plus compétitifs cadrent de manière stricte le déroulement de leurs journées avec des temps incompressibles de récupération, d'entretien physique et de mise en condition psychologique. Mais d'autres ne peuvent le faire. Tu as des obligations, tu sais que si tu es là, c'est parce qu'autour de toi il y a un environnement humain et financier qui s'est construit, alors tu essayes de répondre à ses attentes. C'est ce qui fait la différence entre un partenariat basé sur un projet sportif et compétitif et un autre basé sur un projet, disons, plus opportuniste. Cette course génère beaucoup de retombées auprès du public et certains sponsors y viennent uniquement attirés par cela, sans adhérer pour autant au mythe de cette aventure. Si tu as fait le choix de t'associer avec ce type de partenaire, si tu n'as pas eu le choix faute d'argent pour participer à ce rêve qu'est le Vendée Globe, alors tu joues le rôle que te propose le dircom, être présent jusqu'à l'avant-veille du départ aux soirées de l'entreprise, serrer des mains, expliquer, accueillir, faire le tour du bateau…

Pendant ces semaines, tu rencontres aussi tellement de monde, dans les rues, les cafés, sur le ponton… L'engouement du public te gagne et parfois t'emporte. Tu as envie de remercier, de rendre ces centaines de petits coups de main dont tu as bénéficié tout au long de ta préparation, les sourires, les encouragements, les bénévoles de l'organisation, le public qui s'est déplacé pour te voir et qui va te porter pendant les mois à venir. Tu te dis que tu vas être sérieux, concentré uniquement sur ta préparation, mais devant le sourire d'un gamin ou le questionnement d'une grand-mère, l'envie s'impose de répondre aux sollicitations, d'être présent.

Quand tu as un sponsor, c'est déjà difficile de dire non lorsqu'il te sollicite. Tu le comprends, tu te mets à sa place. Mais lorsque tu as des multi-partenaires… Avec quinze sponsors, c'est quinze fois l'histoire à refaire même s'ils font très attention à ne te demander que le minimum. Deux ou trois jours avant le départ, ça se voyait sur son visage qu'elle était à bout, crevée.

Et c'est le grand jour ! Au petit matin, tu arrives au bateau. Tu gères ton stress et la tension que tu sens sourdre autour de toi. Tu suis le protocole, à l'heure dite, à la minute près, les amarres sont larguées.
Tu descends le chenal avec ces milliers de personnes massées tout du long. Si jamais tu avais évacué la dimension de ce vers quoi tu t'élances, te revoilà dans le bain. Tu peux mettre du temps à résorber les émotions de ce moment. Pour ceux qui l'ont déjà vécu, c'est plus facile à gérer. Mais même avec l'expérience la sortie du port reste toujours un grand moment.

Tu dois être à l'avant de ton bateau pour saluer. Tu lèves les bras, tu regardes les gens, tu veux rendre les signes que l'on t'adresse. Mais le chenal des Sables-d'Olonne, c'est long. Et arrivé au bout, tu n'es même pas en mer que tu as déjà des crampes aux bras.

Enfin en mer, avec ton équipe réduite, tu fais des ronds dans l'eau avant le top départ. Ça dure plusieurs heures. Tu as toujours un truc à fignoler ou une mauvaise surprise à gérer. En 2012, un éolien d'Arnaud Boissières, en tête de mât, arrête de fonctionner juste à la sortie du port. Il en a un second, mais s'il tombe à son tour en rade, ça veut dire qu'il n'aura plus d'infos de vent pendant son tour du monde. Que doit-il faire ? Rentrer au port, réparer et ne pas être présent sur la ligne avec les autres ? Tu imagines ce que ça veut dire louper le départ ? Alors il se dit que les dés sont jetés, qu'il a grillé un joker avant même de partir, mais que le tour du monde est devant lui, en avant ! Et 91 jours plus tard, il boucle la boucle… Chance, son éolien de secours n'a pas lâché. À chaque édition tu as ce genre d'histoires et de dilemmes.

Un premier signal est envoyé : tout le monde doit quitter le bord. C'est extrêmement rapide, tu es avec tes copains et top, tu es seul. Encore quelques ronds dans l'eau, tu te prépares à franchir la ligne. Soit tu joues des coudes pour être en tête, comme en régate, soit tu laisses les cadors à leur affaire et tu regardes la bagarre de derrière. Depuis 2000, à chaque fois, plusieurs bateaux mordent la ligne et doivent la repasser… Trois mois de navigation nous attendent et l'on se bat pour quelques secondes. C'est psychologique, engageant, motivant, un peu fou.

La ligne est passée et c'est la transition, brutale. On bascule. D'un coup, ta concentration focalise l'ensemble de ton cerveau, tu réprimes tes émotions, les bateaux suiveurs, les spectateurs, l'agitation, c'est déjà un autre monde. Il n'y a plus qu'une direction vers laquelle tu te tends : le large.
En quelques minutes, tu es seul, la dimension du tour du monde s'allonge devant toi. L'horizon, cet arc de cercle si fascinant devient une ambition, celle du tour du monde en solitaire.

Et tout ça pompe une énergie de dingue. Au départ du Vendée Globe, tu es crevé.

DESCENDRE L'ATLANTIQUE NORD, CHANGER D'HÉMISPHÈRE, ENTRER DANS L'ATLANTIQUE SUD, PASSER LE CAP DE BONNE-ESPÉRANCE ET VOICI LES MERS DU SUD, TRAVERSER L'OCÉAN INDIEN ET L'OCÉAN PACIFIQUE, SALUER LE CAP HORN ET REMONTER VERS L'EUROPE, À NOUVEAU PAR LES ATLANTIQUES, REVENIR DANS L'HÉMISPHÈRE NORD, ET, PEUT-ÊTRE, DANS QUELQUES MOIS, REVOIR LES SABLES-D'OLONNE.
ATTENDRE LES INDICATIONS DU COMITÉ DE COURSE.
PRB

Maitre CoQ
acciona
BOSS
BOSS
BOSS

UN PREMIER SIGNAL, L'ÉQUIPE QUITTE LE BATEAU.
ET 10 MINUTES APRÈS, **TOP!** C'EST PARTI.
IL N'Y A PAS DE TRANSITION, C'EST IMMÉDIAT, UNE BASCULE, UN NOUVEAU MONDE EST DEVANT LES ÉTRAVES.

« SUR LA LIGNE DE DÉPART, TU OUVRES UN GRAND LIVRE
ET CE N'EST PAS TOI QUI EN ÉCRIS LE SCÉNARIO,
JUSTE DES DÉTAILS ET QUELQUES INFLEXIONS. »

Il n'y a pas de mystère

Samantha Davies – 2008

MAIS TOUT CELA N'A DE SENS QUE SI TU PARVIENS À GARDER TON BATEAU AU MAXIMUM DE SES CAPACITÉS. TU DOIS LE SURVEILLER, L'ENTRETENIR, RÉPARER CHAQUE PETITE CHOSE ET NE RIEN REPORTER AU LENDEMAIN.
ROXY
UNE FOIS EN MER, TA SEULE VARIABLE D'AJUSTEMENT, C'EST TOI. NE JAMAIS T'OUBLIER, PRÉSERVER TON PHYSIQUE ET TON MENTAL. SURTOUT TON MENTAL. ÇA VEUT DIRE MANGER, DORMIR, TE PROTÉGER, ÊTRE DANS L'ANTICIPATION PERMANENTE.
ET POUR TOUT ÇA, MON INGRÉDIENT DE BASE, C'EST LE PLAISIR. PENDANT LE VENDÉE GLOBE, J'ÉTAIS TOUT LE TEMPS HEUREUSE. HEUREUSE D'ÊTRE LÀ OÙ J'ÉTAIS, TOUT LE TEMPS.

Il faut à cela ajouter l'argent qui fait que, définitivement, on ne lutte pas à arme égale. Il faut savoir se vendre, aller chercher les sous, diriger une équipe… Avant on disait que la monotypie, dont le circuit Figaro en est l'excellence, désignait qui était le meilleur marin sur l'eau. Et que pour savoir qui est le ou la meilleure sur l'eau et à terre, il fallait regarder les courses comme le Vendée Globe. On ajoutait que pour réussir ce challenge, il fallait être un artisan aux mille métiers, mais aujourd'hui, parler d'artisanat est dépassé. Pour être en tête de flotte, il faut aussi savoir naviguer dans le monde de l'entrepreneuriat, du management, de la communication… sans oublier, bien sûr, de toujours être excellent en mer.

Seul, enfin, et il faut vite te mettre la tête à l'endroit, physiquement éponger les jours du départ, parce que la météo n'attend pas et la course se passe déjà devant toi. Tu cavales pour la rattraper et même quand tu es premier, tu as l'impression de cavaler après tu ne sais trop quoi tellement ça va vite. "Ça part par-devant", c'est une vérité générale, alors il faut y aller et ne pas lâcher la tête. "Les riches s'enrichissent et les pauvres s'appauvrissent", sur des courses aussi longues, le dicton est au goût du jour, alors reste du bon côté.

On était à 50 milles l'un de l'autre. Je lui ai envoyé un message -- On va prendre cher. Et quand elle m'a répondu, c'était pour me dire qu'elle venait de démâter. On était au large du cap Finistère, ça commençait dur.

Pour le Vendée Globe, le "bon marin" n'est pas celui ou celle qui sait le mieux jouer avec ses voiles, appréhender la mer, anticiper le vent, en un mot, naviguer. Non. Le bon marin, le ou la meilleure, c'est celui ou celle qui sait faire tout cela et qui, en plus, sait imaginer le bateau le mieux adapté au parcours et à sa propre personnalité, ses caractéristiques. Le Vendée Globe ne se court pas en monotypie, on n'a pas chacun un bateau identique. On est sur celui qui correspond à notre philosophie de navigation. Sur un tour du monde, tu vas enchaîner toutes les conditions de mer et de vent, et toi-même, tu vas passer par tous les états, du plus optimiste au plus pessimiste, du plus flamboyant au plus amorphe, de l'euphorie à l'abattement. Il n'existe pas un bateau qui sera le plus performant dans toutes les conditions, ni qui réussira à associer confort et performance. Il y a des choix et des compromis à faire. C'est, en plus d'être un bon marin sur l'eau, ce que juge une course comme le Vendée Globe.

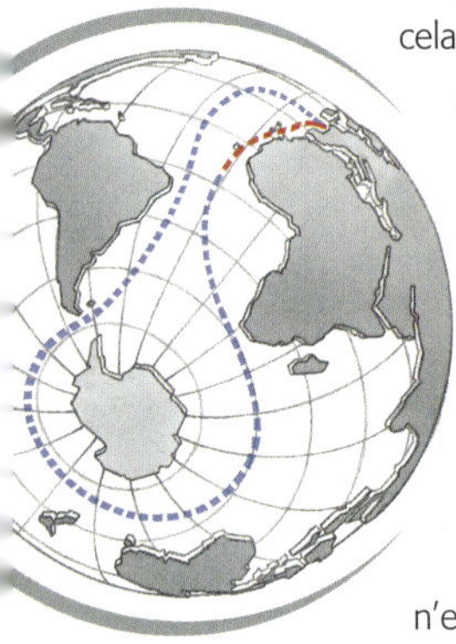

Dans les premiers jours, tu as souvent l'abandon de ceux ou celles qui n'étaient pas vraiment prêts ou qui ont eu un très gros coup de malchance. En 2012, Marc Guillemot, sur un des bateaux techniquement les plus aboutis de la flotte, perd sa quille après 4 heures et 43 minutes de course… Ou lorsque tu percutes un chalutier qui ne se signale pas au radar et navigue tous feux éteints, c'est comme jouer à la roulette russe.

En 2012, Le Cléac'h, Riou, Gabart, qui avaient navigué à bloc sur leur bateau les trois années précédentes, sont partis comme des fusées. Aux autres de s'accrocher, normal.

L'autre scénario, c'est la tempête. Sur la façade atlantique française, en hiver, c'est un cas météo fréquent. En 2012, ça s'est plutôt bien passé car même si ça a pas mal bastonné, on a eu quelques heures après la ligne pour s'y préparer, pour se mettre dans le bain. Mais en 2008, c'est un gros coup de tabac qui, d'entrée de jeu, nous accueille, avec une mer désordonnée, très creuse. Souvent, on se dit que ce n'est "que" le Gascogne, mais les marins de l'autre côté du monde appellent la pointe d'Ouessant le Cap Horn de l'Europe... Il y en a quand même pas mal qui ont fini là leur course.

Je fais un super golfe de Gascogne et au cap Finistère, je suis assez bien placé. Mais au large du Portugal, c'est le coup de mou. Je fais un premier empannage au bon endroit, au bon moment. Là, Le Cam, je l'ai à vue. Mais après, crevé, manque de lucidité, je réempanne, je me décale de 20 milles vers l'est... et je me retrouve déventé. Ces 20 milles d'écart, 10 jours après à l'équateur, ça devient 300 milles et je tire la langue.

Après le golfe de Gascogne, tu atteins le cap Finistère, la pointe nord-ouest de l'Espagne. Et déjà ici, tu peux acter, pour les mois à venir, qui sera dans le rythme de la course et qui va ramer tout du long pour rattacher les wagons. Ça n'est pas rare de voir un skipper ne pas réussir à se hisser au classement au minimum de là où on l'attendait. Psychologiquement, ça fait mal de courir après sa propre course. Il en faut de la ressource mentale pour ne pas lâcher.

Toute cette période est assez technique, on est dans une anticipation à longue échéance. On réfléchit déjà à là où l'on veut entrer dans le Pot-au-Noir, cette bande sans vent positionnée peu avant l'équateur. Il reste pourtant plusieurs jours avant de l'atteindre, longer le Portugal, le Maroc, le Sahara, la Mauritanie...

Pendant tout ce temps, c'est difficile d'expliquer au public ce que l'on fait et pourquoi on le fait. Entre l'enjeu tactique de se taire et le besoin de se construire son espace solitaire, "prendre la mer et son bateau", peu de skippers communiquent spontanément. Pour le public, ça donne une saveur un peu fade à la course alors qu'on n'en est qu'au début de l'aventure. C'est moche pour l'engouement populaire et pourtant, nous sur les bateaux, on est déjà au taquet.

C'est au bout de 3, 4 jours que je me sens bien. Quand tu t'es fait à l'idée que c'est parti pour trois mois, tout seul, que tu coupes les ponts avec la terre.

BELLE MER, BEAU TEMPS AU LARGE DU BRÉSIL.
DELTA DORE
BANG !
DELTA DORE
?!
QU'EST-CE QUE…

NOOON !!
OOOOH...
ALLÔ, SYLVAIN ?
JE N'AI EU BESOIN QUE DU BRUIT ET D'UN COUP D'ŒIL À TRAVERS LE HUBLOT POUR SAVOIR.
C'EST FOUTU, JE VAIS DEVOIR ABANDONNER.

ATTENDS ! TU ES EN SÉCURITÉ ?
OUI.
LE BATEAU EST À L'ENDROIT ?
OUI.
IL N'Y A PAS DE VOIE D'EAU ?
NON.
LE MÂT EST TOUJOURS DEBOUT ?
OUI.
ALORS RIEN N'EST JOUÉ.
TU AS DU MATÉRIEL DE RECHANGE, UNE BONNE MÉTÉO ET ON EST LÀ.
ON VA TROUVER. TU VAS ME DÉCRIRE LA SITUATION. TU DOIS GARDER LE MORAL. UNE SOLUTION DOIT EXISTER. ELLE DOIT EXISTER. C'EST ÇA QU'IL FAUT QUE TU AIES EN TÊTE.
ON VA PROCÉDER MÉTHODIQUEMENT, PAR ORDRE. LES CHOSES LES UNES APRÈS LES AUTRES.
PREMIÈREMENT. LE BATEAU AVANCE TOUJOURS ?
OUI.
TU ES À QUELLE ALLURE ?
AU PORTANT.
QUEL CAP ?
EUUH... 195°...
MAIS ÇA N'A PLUS TROP D'IMPORTANCE MAINTENANT...
DELTA DORE
35
SYLVAIN, ARRÊTE S'IL TE PLAÎT. IL FAUT QUE TU M'ÉCOUTES. JE SUIS EN TRAIN DE REGARDER LA CARTE. JE VAIS PRENDRE TROIS JOURS AU MOINS POUR REJOINDRE LE BRÉSIL.
TANT QUE JE RESTE SUR LE MÊME BORD, ÇA VA, IL N'Y A PAS DE DANGER. UNE FOIS PRÈS DE LA CÔTE, JE VAIS AVOIR BESOIN DE VOTRE AIDE. VOUS POUVEZ ÊTRE EN COMBIEN DE TEMPS À RECIFE ? TU AS DES CONTACTS LÀ-BAS ?
JÉRÉM' ! TU ME DIS DE T'ÉCOUTER. OK. MAIS LA LOGISTIQUE, ON S'EN FOUT. TU ME DIS QUE C'EST FOUTU, OK. JE VEUX BIEN L'ENTENDRE...
MAIS BORDEL ! TU VAS ME DIRE CE QUI SE PASSE ?!
... EXCUSE-MOI.
LA SITUATION EST CLAIRE, MAIS LES IDÉES S'ENTRECHOQUENT UN PEU...
IL Y A EU UN GRAND BANG ! AU NIVEAU DU MÂT. J'AI VU PAR LE HUBLOT SOUS LE VENT LA BARRE DE FLÈCHE N°2 SE BALADER, PENDUE AU HAUBAN. ELLE NE RETIENT PLUS LE MÂT.
AH...
OK...
JE VAIS SORTIR FAIRE UN DIAGNOSTIC PLUS PRÉCIS. JE TE RAPPELLE APRÈS.

UNE FOIS DEHORS, LE CONSTAT N'EST QUE CONFIRMATION DE CE QUE J'AVAIS ENTENDU, SENTI, APERÇU. LE HAUBAN EST COMPLÈTEMENT CHIBRÉ, TIRE-BOUCHONNÉ, ET LA BARRE DE FLÈCHE IRRÉPARABLE.
L'AIR ÉTAIT FRAIS, VIVIFIANT.
LE CIEL BLEU, PUR. C'ÉTAIT UNE BIEN BELLE JOURNÉE.
UNE DE CELLES OÙ RIEN NE PEUT ARRIVER, OÙ RIEN NE DOIT ARRIVER. SAUF L'IMPRÉVU QUI TOUCHE UNE DES MILLE PETITES PIÈCES QUI FONT NOS BATEAUX, SI PERFORMANTS ET SI COMPLEXES.
C'ÉTAIT VRAIMENT UNE TROP BELLE JOURNÉE.
LE 26 NOVEMBRE 2008, ALORS QU'IL NAVIGUAIT DANS LE PAQUET DE TÊTE, JÉRÉMIE BEYOU ANNONCE SON ABANDON.

À la sortie du Pot-au-Noir, le départ est soldé depuis un moment, en bien ou en mal, et la flotte n'est plus homogène. Tu vois qui sera devant, qui sera au milieu et qui sera derrière, elle s'est divisée par "paquets". Si tu regardes le Vendée Globe comme une entité unique, tu passes à côté des débats. Pour chaque paquet, ce sont des raisonnements différents qui vont motiver les skippers. Au classement, l'ordre entre les divisions est déjà plus ou moins joué, mais celui au sein de chaque division va faire l'objet d'âpres bagarres. Des bagarres qui vont se jouer à l'échelle d'un océan, voire de deux ou trois.

Si tu es en première division, ton but est d'être sur la plus haute marche du podium. Tu as un gros budget, un bateau neuf ou le top de l'avant-dernière génération, et tu espères que tes compromis performance-fiabilisation ont été les bons. La performance, c'est la légèreté, l'innovation, la pièce que tu fais évoluer jusqu'au dernier moment. La fiabilisation, c'est de tester en mer chaque élément, de lui faire subir des conditions changeantes et dures. C'est accepter un peu plus de poids pour renforcer une pièce peut-être au-delà du besoin. La performance et la fiabilisation souvent s'opposent.

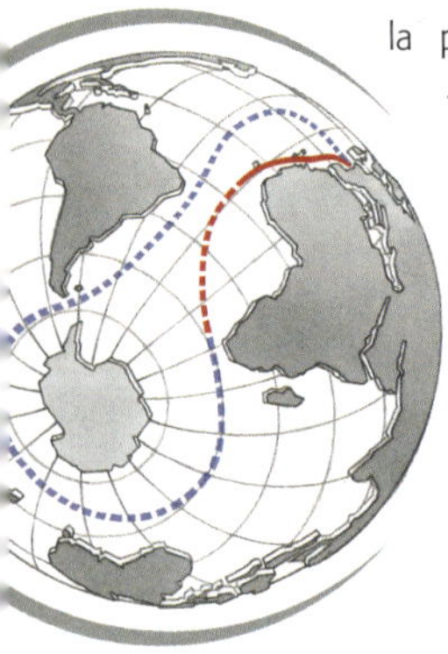

Tu vas maintenant naviguer en fonction de ton positionnement et de ta personnalité. Soit prendre des options, être joueur, vouloir décrocher les autres, soit au contraire être dans le contrôle de tes adversaires, dans le gain assuré, ne pas commettre d'erreurs plutôt que de tenter de gagner des points. Tes yeux pleurent à force de comparer ton compteur de vitesse et ton tableau de polaires, les vitesses maximales à atteindre en fonction des conditions de vent et de mer que tu as établies et mises à jour au cours de tes navigations d'entraînement.

À l'extrême rigueur, si un bateau se détache particulièrement, tu feras peut-être une croix sur la première place, mais avec beaucoup de regret et seulement si tu n'as pas cassé avant de t'être fait à l'idée... Et dans ce cas, les deuxième ou troisième places vont valoir très, très cher et plus nombreux encore en seront les prétendants.

Tu navigues mieux avec un bateau pas loin de toi que lorsque tu es tout seul. Mais c'est dangereux aussi parce que tu tires sur la bête. Et lorsque tu arrives à te tempérer, tu essayes que l'autre dépasse sa frontière performance-casse. Tu joues à "vas-y, éclate-moi" en espérant qu'il va tout péter.

En deuxième division, tu aimerais jouer la gagne, tu en as peut-être les capacités physiques et mentales, mais tu n'as pas le bateau pour. Ton but est d'être le mieux placé au classement final. Alors ta première considération est que pour être bien classé, il faut être classé avant tout. Finir ton Vendée Globe aux Sables-d'Olonne est ton premier objectif, tu te répètes qu'il faut que tu envoies mais en sachant ne pas dépasser les moyennes maximales que tu t'es fixées. Avec ton budget, tu as soit misé sur la performance, et ça va être difficile de ne pas casser avec toutes les pièces que tu n'as pas pu changer faute d'argent, soit tu as fiabilisé ta machine et tu as toutes les cartes en main pour couper la ligne d'arrivée, mais tu risques d'évoluer dans le ventre mou de la course, au milieu ou à l'arrière de ta division.
Pour qui analyse les trajectoires des bateaux de cette division, quelques hauts faits de la navigation au large se déroulent ici. Des paris météo osés, des bateaux qui se font manger par d'autres de générations beaucoup plus anciennes, des réparations techniques qui prouvent que le luxe n'est pas toujours la panacée, des chevauchées solitaires longues d'un océan... Humainement, la deuxième division révèle des moments magnifiques.

Tu attends chaque fois les classements avec le palpitant, voir si ton coup a réussi. Et si tu as l'impression d'avoir bombardé, tu regardes les positions des autres bateaux et... alors, est-ce que je les largue ?

En troisième division, tu retrouves des bateaux qui ne sont plus dans les critères techniques du moment et des skippers pas forcément régatiers. Être sur la ligne de départ est souvent le plus grand exploit de ton Vendée Globe. Tu vas naviguer intelligemment, te concentrer sur toutes les casses qui ne manqueront pas de venir agrémenter ton tour du monde. Tu sais qu'avec raison tu devrais boucler la boucle. Tu vas faire des paris sur des objectifs en rapport avec ton navire. Le bateau à dépasser, c'est le tien. Et le classement? Une cerise sur le gâteau. Alessandro di Benedetto, en 2012, il arrive dernier, mais il arrive 12e sur 30 au départ, c'est pas mal non?

Et enfin, il y a la quatrième division. C'est une division extra-sportive où la communication et la publicité ont pris le pas sur ce que représente ce tour du monde. On n'y joue pas le jeu de la compétition, de l'engagement, du "faire au mieux". Faire avancer son bateau "au mieux", développer une stratégie "au mieux", sans relâche se donner, relever le challenge qui est de tourner autour du monde, seul et sans assistance, le plus rapidement possible selon tes capacités et celles de ton bateau. La beauté du Vendée Globe s'épanouit pourtant dans cette quête. Ne pas s'y atteler, c'est dommageable pour la course, pour les skippers, pour le public et aussi pour les sponsors présents sur le long terme.
Que des skippers s'engagent dans cette voie, comment les en blâmer... Tu rêves du Vendée Globe et un beau jour, on te propose d'y aller dans de bonnes conditions. Car ne nous y trompons pas, ces bateaux ne sont pas les moins bien lotis, ils ont de beaux budgets... alors comment refuser?

Pour moi, ces bateaux s'apparentent plus à la caravane du Tour de France. C'est le cirque ! Les vidéos envoyées du bord, c'est comme si on t'envoyait un saucisson, une casquette, un maillot publicitaire. On s'exhibe, c'est à celui qui aura fait le meilleur tour de piste... On n'est plus du tout dans la compétition sportive, ni dans ce qu'est le Vendée Globe.

Nous pourrions faire en sorte que le Vendée Globe soit financièrement plus accessible, contrôler les coûts, mais alors fini la recherche, l'innovation, la création de bateaux. Et puis poser de nouveaux cadres, édicter de nouvelles règles, toujours plus, toujours plus... Être seul, en mer, sans assistance, l'essence de la course, alors tant pis.

Mais quelle que soit ta division, l'un des juges de la compétition sera la casse. Chaque abandon va faire monter des bateaux au classement. Le haut de la deuxième division intègre parfois le top 5 et bon an, mal an, 50 % des bateaux jettent l'éponge.
François Gabart estime que le Vendée Globe ne se gagne pas, mais plutôt qu'il ne se perd pas. Et il sait de quoi il parle, il ne l'a pas perdu lors de l'édition 2012... À quelques exceptions près, l'histoire de la course lui donne raison. Celui ou celle qui aura commis le moins d'erreurs sera sur la plus haute marche du podium. Et encore, il ou elle dira qu'il ou qu'elle a eu "un peu de réussite". Assurément il en faut plus que de coutume pour y parvenir, car déjà, arriver au bout, en réclame une sacrée dose.

Une nuit aux Açores, 400 milles dans l'Indien

Roland Jourdain et Vincent Riou – 2004

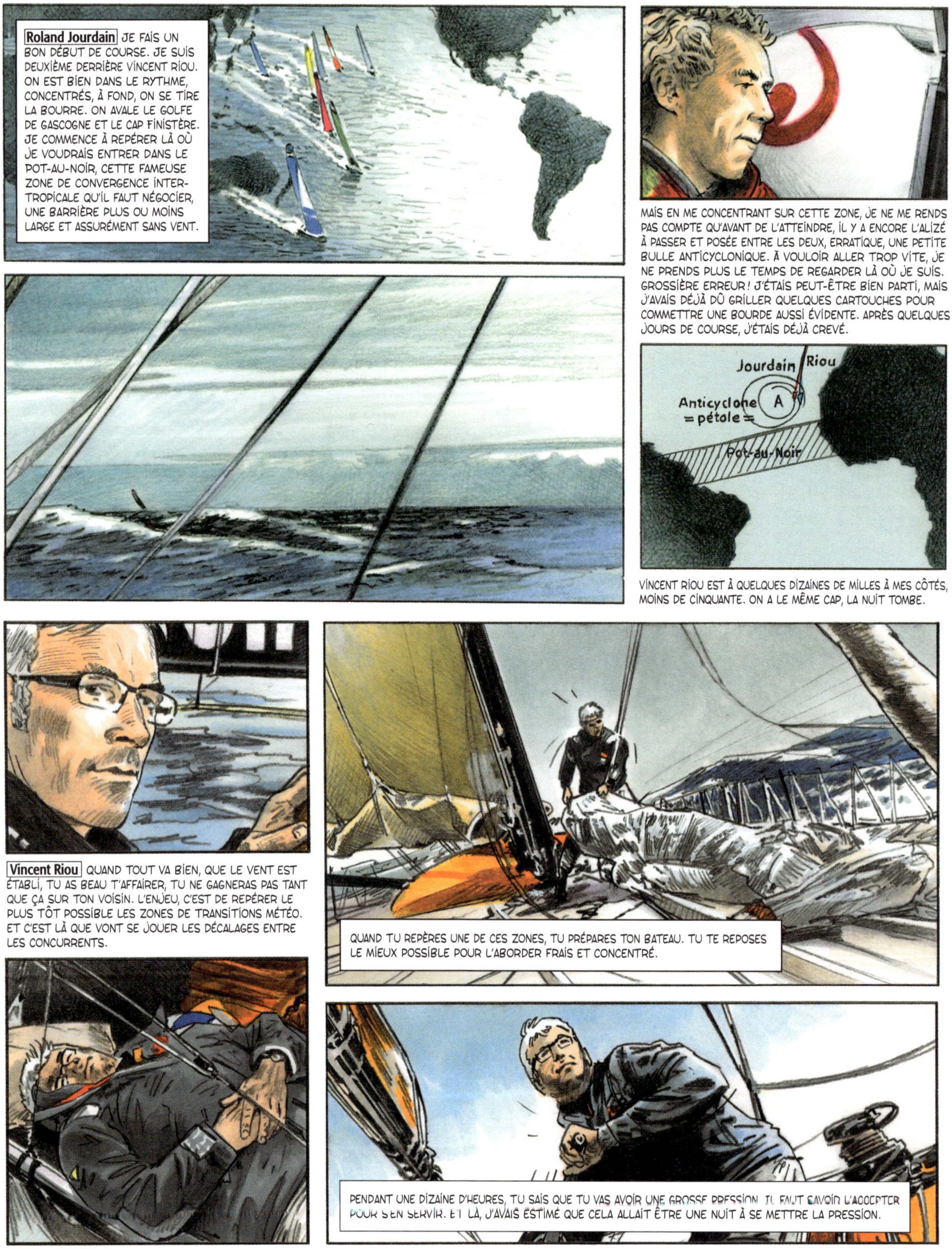

Jourdain PENDANT LA NUIT, LE VENT TOMBE. LE STRESS! JE ME SUIS TROP RAPPROCHÉ DE L'ANTICYCLONE. ET LES PROCHAINS RELEVÉS DE POSITIONS SONT AU PETIT MATIN. JE NE PEUX QU'ATTENDRE ET À L'HEURE DITE, JE ME RUE SUR LES FICHIERS. VINCENT A MIS 10° DANS SON CAP! IL A ÉVITÉ LA MOLLE ET FILE DEVANT ALORS QUE JE SUIS ENGLUÉ DANS LA PÉTOLE!
AAAAH!
C'EST L'HORREUR TOTALE. IL N'Y A RIEN DE PLUS DUR DANS LA VIE. JE SUIS EFFONDRÉ. ENFIN… IL NE FAUT PAS PARTIR EN VRILLE ET PERDRE CONTACT AVEC LA RÉALITÉ… IL Y A DES MILLIARDS DE PERSONNES QUI SONT PLUS MALHEUREUSES QUE MOI À CE MOMENT-LÀ. TU N'ES VRAIMENT PAS À PLAINDRE… MAIS PARFOIS, DANS LE STRESS, IL N'Y A PLUS QUE TON MONDE QUI EXISTE. ET LÀ, TU NE PEUX PAS, MAIS TU NE PEUX PAS TE RAISONNER. TU NE PEUX PAS! JE SUIS BLOQUÉ À NE RIEN POUVOIR FAIRE. ET JE VOIS SUR LA CARTOGRAPHIE VINCENT QUI S'EN VA, QUI S'EN VA, QUI S'EN VA…
Jourdain
Riou
Anticyclone
A
Pot-au-Noir
Le Cam
Golding
A
Pot-au-Noir
MIKE GOLDING, QUI ÉTAIT JUSTE DERRIÈRE, SE PLANTE DANS LA MÊME PÉTOLE QUE MOI. ET JEAN LE CAM, QUI ARRIVE PAR-DERRIÈRE, TRANQUILLE, IL FAIT LE TOUR DE LA BULLE PAR L'AUTRE CÔTÉ. ET LUI AUSSI IL S'EN VA PAR-DEVANT. SANS MOI! C'EST HORRIBLE. JE ME SENS COMME UN CONDAMNÉ. ET JE NE PEUX EN VOULOIR QU'À MOI-MÊME, C'EST UNE PURE ERREUR DE STRATÉGIE.
YES!
Riou TU REGARDES LA CARTE ET TU AS LE MORAL TOUT LÀ-HAUT. DES COUPS DE FATIGUE COMME ÇA, TU EN REDEMANDES, C'EST LE MEILLEUR STIMULANT.
UN ANTICYCLONE, C'EST COMME UNE PATATE. ENTRE SON CENTRE ET LA POINTE DE SON EXTENSION, IL Y A UNE BARRIÈRE SANS VENT. SI TU ARRIVES À LA PASSER EN PREMIER, IL Y A DE FORTES CHANCES POUR QUE TU T'ÉCHAPPES PAR-DEVANT.
J'AVAIS UN BATEAU POLYVALENT ET TRÈS FIABILISÉ. J'AVAIS PU ME PERMETTRE DE PARTIR LÉGER. JOURDAIN ET LE CAM AVAIENT DES BATEAUX PLUS RÉCENTS, PLUS PUISSANTS, PLUS RAPIDES AU PORTANT, MAIS PAR PETIT TEMPS…

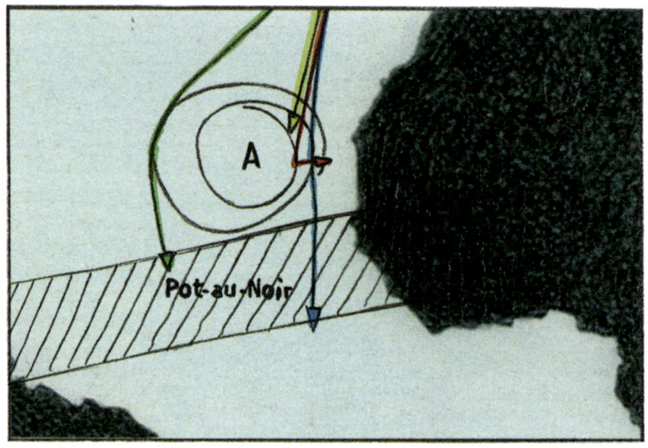

Jourdain C'EST FICHU, ILS SONT PARTIS, IL FAUT QUE JE ME BOUGE. ALORS JE PRENDS UNE DÉCISION PAS ÉVIDENTE : JE PARS À 90° DE MA ROUTE. IL FAUDRAIT QUE J'AILLE AU SUD, VERS L'ÉQUATEUR, ET JE METS LE CAP SUR L'AFRIQUE, PLEIN EST.

VINCENT ET JEAN ONT EU LE TEMPS DE PASSER EN COUPANT AU PLUS COURT. JE PRENDS DOUBLE PEINE !

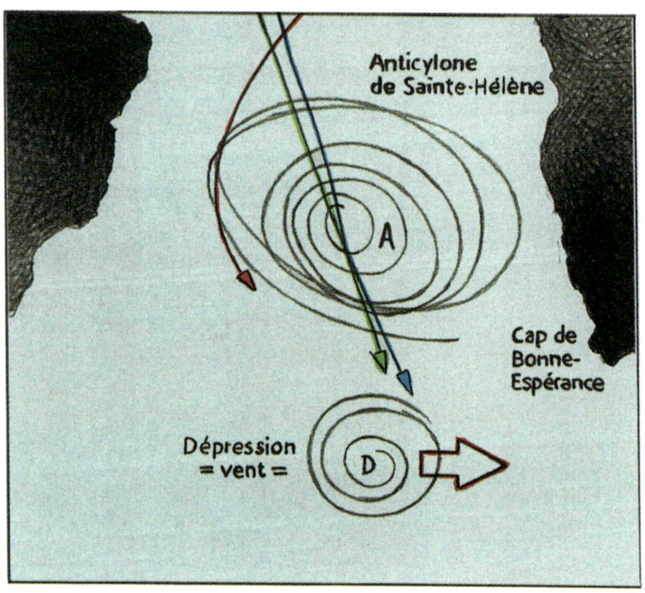

LE BUT EN DESCENDANT L'ATLANTIQUE, C'EST D'ATTRAPER AVANT TOUT LE MONDE UNE DES DÉPRESSIONS QUI TOURNENT AUTOUR DE L'ANTARCTIQUE. C'EST COMME POUR LES TRAINS : SI TU N'ATTRAPES PAS CELUI-LÀ, TU PRENDRAS LE SUIVANT... ET TU ARRIVERAS PLUS TARD.

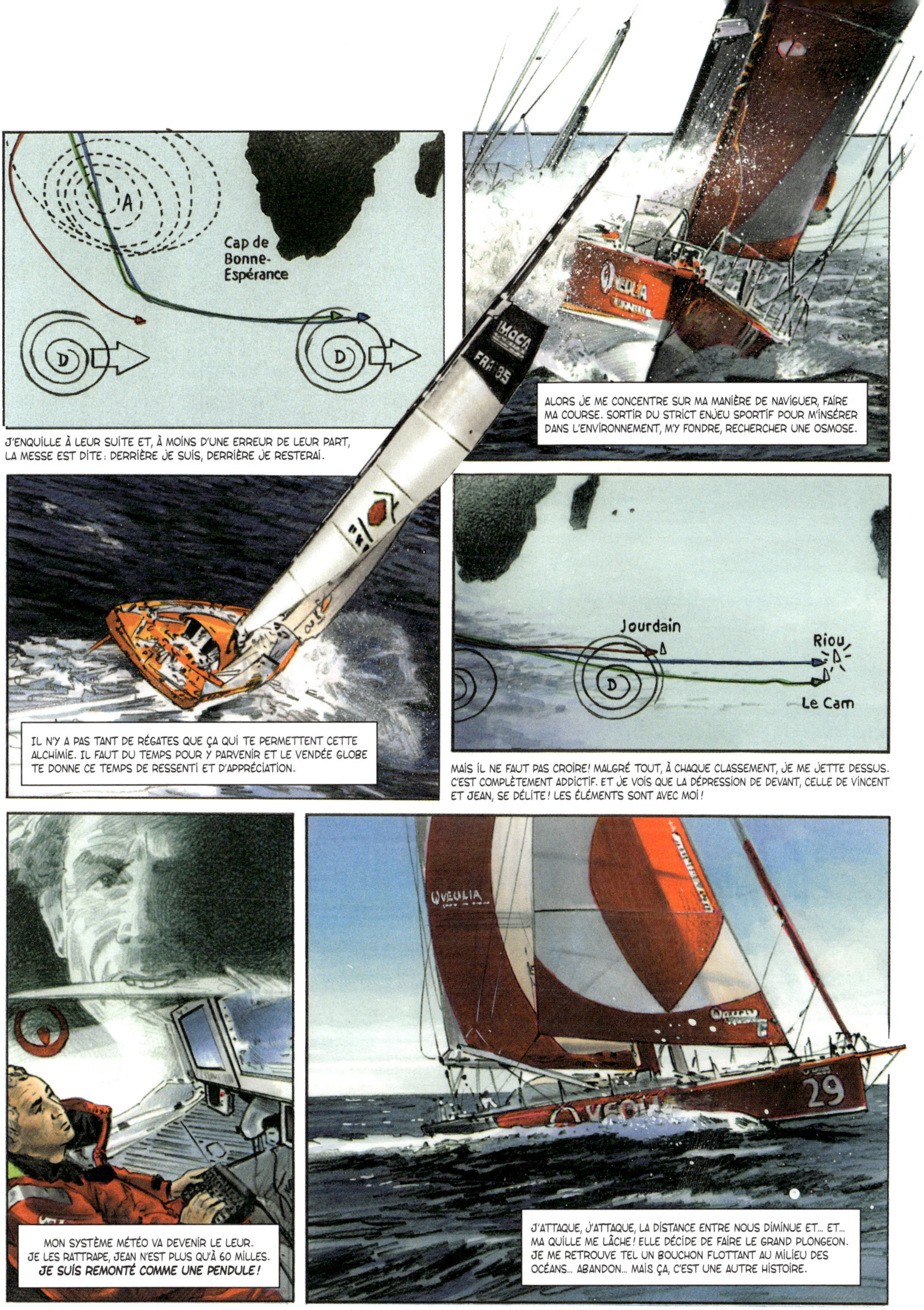
A
Cap de Bonne-Espérance
D
D
J'ENQUILLE À LEUR SUITE ET, À MOINS D'UNE ERREUR DE LEUR PART, LA MESSE EST DITE : DERRIÈRE JE SUIS, DERRIÈRE JE RESTERAI.
ALORS JE ME CONCENTRE SUR MA MANIÈRE DE NAVIGUER, FAIRE MA COURSE. SORTIR DU STRICT ENJEU SPORTIF POUR M'INSÉRER DANS L'ENVIRONNEMENT, M'Y FONDRE, RECHERCHER UNE OSMOSE.
IL N'Y A PAS TANT DE RÉGATES QUE ÇA QUI TE PERMETTENT CETTE ALCHIMIE. IL FAUT DU TEMPS POUR Y PARVENIR ET LE VENDÉE GLOBE TE DONNE CE TEMPS DE RESSENTI ET D'APPRÉCIATION.
Jourdain
Riou
D
Le Cam
MAIS IL NE FAUT PAS CROIRE ! MALGRÉ TOUT, À CHAQUE CLASSEMENT, JE ME JETTE DESSUS. C'EST COMPLÈTEMENT ADDICTIF. ET JE VOIS QUE LA DÉPRESSION DE DEVANT, CELLE DE VINCENT ET JEAN, SE DÉLITE ! LES ÉLÉMENTS SONT AVEC MOI !
MON SYSTÈME MÉTÉO VA DEVENIR LE LEUR. JE LES RATTRAPE, JEAN N'EST PLUS QU'À 60 MILLES. ***JE SUIS REMONTÉ COMME UNE PENDULE !***
29
J'ATTAQUE, J'ATTAQUE, LA DISTANCE ENTRE NOUS DIMINUE ET… ET… MA QUILLE ME LÂCHE ! ELLE DÉCIDE DE FAIRE LE GRAND PLONGEON. JE ME RETROUVE TEL UN BOUCHON FLOTTANT AU MILIEU DES OCÉANS… ABANDON… MAIS ÇA, C'EST UNE AUTRE HISTOIRE.

06:00
HEY!!
MERDE! LE PILOTE NE RÉPOND PAS, LE BATEAU RESTE COUCHÉ.
INVERSER LA QUILLE, ELLE VA FAIRE BALANCIER. IL N'Y AURA PLUS QUE LES VOILES QUI NOUS RETIENDRONT À PLAT.
06:03
PAS DE PRÉCIPITATION. N'ALLONS PAS AGGRAVER LA SITUATION.

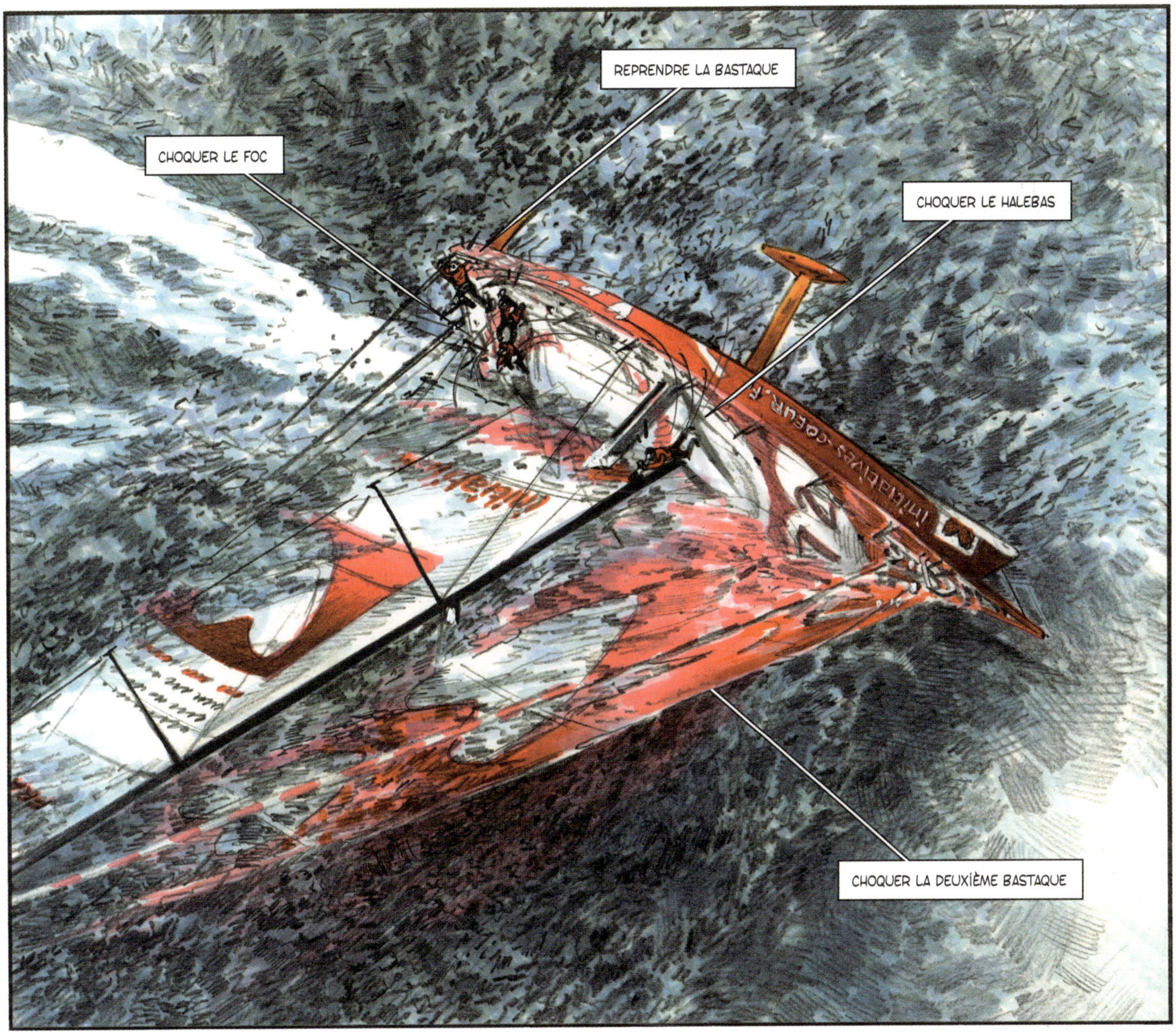
CHOQUER LE FOC
REPRENDRE LA BASTAQUE
CHOQUER LE HALEBAS
CHOQUER LA DEUXIÈME BASTAQUE

07:10
ENCORE L'ÉCOUTE À REPRENDRE, LES BALLASTS À TRANSFÉRER ET ÇA DEVRAIT SE REDRESSER.

MAIS SANS ATTENDRE...
NOOON! PAS TOUT DE SUITE! JE NE SUIS PAS PRÊT, RESTE ENCORE COUCHÉ UN PETIT PEU!...
CLACK
CLACK
CLACK
CLACK
?
QU'EST-CE QUI PÈTE LE LONG DU MÂT?
... CONTRE MA VOLONTÉ, LE BATEAU SE REDRESSE...
VLAM!!
... ET LA GRAND-VOILE PASSE BRUTALEMENT D'UN BORD À L'AUTRE.
DES LATTES ONT CASSÉ, MAIS ÇA A L'AIR PLUS GRAVE QUE ÇA!
TOUT AFFALER!
ON VERRA APRÈS.
www.initiatives-coeur.fr
07:33

07:39
LE BATEAU FAIT UNE NOUVELLE EMBARDÉE. JE N'AI TOUJOURS PAS RÉGLÉ LE PROBLÈME DÉCLENCHEUR. JE SUIS EN TRAIN DE GÉRER LE SUR-ACCIDENT.
HÉ!
LE PILOTE S'EST DÉCONNECTÉ. PLUS RIEN NE CONTRÔLE LA BARRE.
VITE! ON VA REPARTIR AU TAS.
08:04
C'EST JUSTE LA GOUPILLE QUI A SAUTÉ. REMBOÎTER ET SERRER L'ENSEMBLE. C'EST BON.
LE BATEAU VA ÊTRE STABLE. MAINTENANT À LA GRAND-VOILE, QU'EST-CE QUI LUI EST ARRIVÉ ?
08:12
LES CHARIOTS ONT EXPLOSÉ EN MÊME TEMPS QUE LES LATTES.
PAS DE SOUCI, J'EN AI DE RECHAN...
?!
... ON S'EST PLANTÉS DANS LE MATOS ! CE N'EST PAS LE BON DIAMÈTRE.
08:23
OOOOH...
LÀ, ÇA COMMENCE À SENTIR MAUVAIS.

ALLÔ ! SALUT, BRUNO. JE TE FAIS UN TOPO DE LA SITUATION. J'AI UN SOUCI QUI SE CORSE. J'AURAIS BESOIN DE TON AIDE. JE SUIS PARTI AU TAS, LE PILOTE A DÉCROCHÉ. CE N'EST PAS GRAVE, C'ÉTAIT JUSTE LA GOUPILLE ENTRE LE MOTEUR ET LE BRAS DE LIAISON. PAR CONTRE LE BATEAU A EMPANNÉ D'UN COUP. LES LATTES NE SONT PAS PASSÉES ET DES PINNES DE CHARIOTS ONT CASSÉ. ÇA NON PLUS CE N'EST PAS GRAVE ! CE QUI EST GRAVE, C'EST QU'ON S'EST TROMPÉS DANS LA PRÉPARATION DU MATÉRIEL DE RECHANGE. LES PINNES N'ONT NI LE BON DIAMÈTRE, NI LA BONNE LONGUEUR ! JE NE VOIS PAS DE SOLUTION ET JE COMMENCE À FATIGUER. EST-CE QU'AVEC L'ÉQUIPE, TU PEUX COGITER SUR TOUT ÇA ? DE MON CÔTÉ IL FAUT QUE JE RÉCUPÈRE UN MINIMUM. JE VAIS MANGER, PEUT-ÊTRE QUE ÇA FERA VENIR LES IDÉES.
09:48
HUM...
10:00
BON... **AU BOULOT.**
11:32
16:00
ÇA DEVRAIT LE FAIRE.
BRUNO ? ÇA Y EST : CHANTIER TERMINÉ. J'AI SCIÉ LES ÉCROUS AU NIVEAU DU FILETAGE. J'AI RÉTRÉCI LE DIAMÈTRE AVEC DE LA RÉSINE. C'EST EN TRAIN DE SÉCHER. JE VAIS POUVOIR REMONTER LE PUZZLE.

17:30
LES NOUVEAUX CHARIOTS SONT INSTALLÉS. IL N'Y A PLUS QU'À MOULINER EN ESPÉRANT QUE ÇA TIENNE.
VOILE MONTÉE DE MOITIÉ ET ÇA A L'AIR DE FONCTIONNER. ALLEZ, ENCORE UN EFFORT.
VOILE HAUTE !
LES CHARIOTS SONT TOUS EN TENSION, LES LATTES BIEN RÉGULIÈRES.
JE SUIS VANNÉ, ALLONS-Y CALMEMENT. ON VA BORDER DOUCEMENT.
18:15
6 NŒUDS...
12 NŒUDS...
ÇA TIENT...
YES !
CE N'ÉTAIT QUE MON DEUXIÈME JOUR DANS LE GRAND SUD... UNE ENTRÉE EN MATIÈRE...

Les mers du Sud, on commence à être nombreux à y être allés. En même temps, ramené au nombre de voileux, ça ne fait pas tant que ça. Les bateaux de plaisance n'y sont pas légion et les courses ou records qui t'emmènent par là-bas se comptent sur les doigts d'une main. Quant aux bateaux de commerce, il n'y a rien à gagner à passer par là. La longueur de la houle, sa régularité et son aspect rangé – sauf quand ça souffle vraiment trop, trop fort –, la longévité et la tenue des dépressions, sans même penser aux distances à parcourir et à l'isolement, font que les mers du Sud, ça reste un graal.
Tu descends l'Atlantique et tu arrives en vue de l'autoroute. Clignotant à gauche, tu prends la bretelle qui enroule l'Afrique du Sud et là, tout change d'échelle.

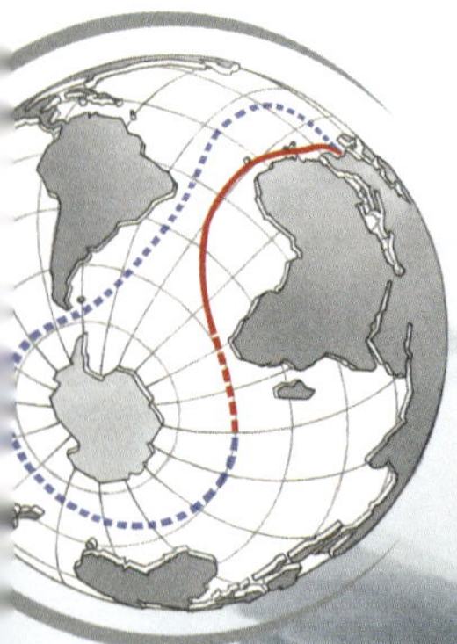

Pour faire simple, le vent se lève au-dessus de la pampa argentine et part vers l'est. Arrivé au-dessus de l'eau, il accélère, accélère, accélère. Il coupe l'océan Atlantique, traverse l'océan Indien et le voilà dans le Pacifique où il continue sa chevauchée jusqu'à rencontrer le seul obstacle sur son passage : le Chili et sa cordillère des Andes. On est déjà au Cap Horn. On vient de faire le tour du monde en ne rencontrant aucune terre avec ce vent qui accélère, accélère, accélère. Et la houle adopte la même dimension.
Dans le Sud, tu es plus petit, plus fragile, plus vulnérable, et c'est ce qui en fait cet espace si unique et grandiose.

Le plus dur, c'est le mouvement perpétuel, t'as envie que ça s'arrête. Mais ça ne s'arrête pas. Il faut attendre d'avoir passé le Cap Horn pour ça.

Tu attrapes une dépression en atteignant les 40es, ceux que l'on appelle les rugissants, et tu essayes de t'y tenir le plus longtemps possible. Si elle te lâche ou si tu ne la tiens pas, tu attends la suivante et tu continues, toujours à fond. Avec nos bateaux qui vont de plus en plus vite, on arrive à rester dans un même système de plus en plus longtemps.

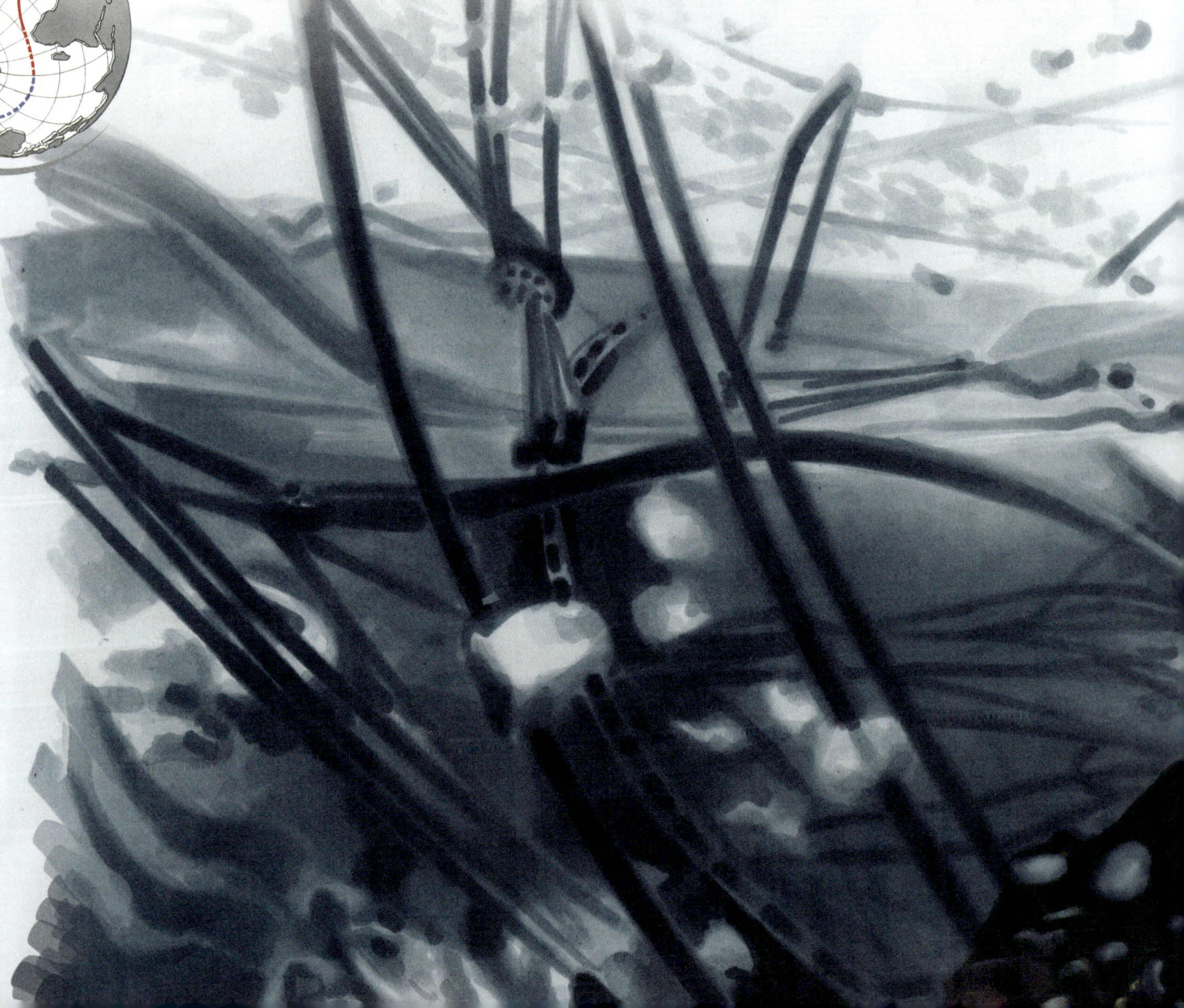

Tu ne fais pas beaucoup de changement de voile, mais pour la moindre manœuvre, tu dépenses énormément de calories. Il y a le froid et le stress… Tu dois encore plus être dans l'anticipation, planifier chaque chose.

Les dépressions sont plus ou moins joufflues avec une houle plus ou moins creuse. Quand tout va bien, ce n'est pas une ambiance agressive, ça ne déferle pas, ce n'est pas abrupt. Ça peut être vallonné, tout en courbes, tu montes, tu descends, avec fluidité. Ça peut être très doux les mers du Sud. Quand ça va moins bien par contre, que ça se fâche, que les collines se raidissent, alors apprête-toi à vivre à quatre pattes, sors les crampons et les pioches. On est plusieurs à mettre un casque pour sortir.

Ici, la course se joue surtout sur les erreurs que tu fais ou que tu ne fais pas, les allures ne sont techniquement pas compliquées. Celui qui sort par-devant est celui qui en aura fait moins que les voisins. Là, il faut savoir bien naviguer, mais il faut aussi avoir du métier.

En 2008, l'édition avait été salée, on se prenait dépression sur dépression avec des vents à 60 nœuds. Je me souviens des messages envoyés par Le Cam et Riou, pas vraiment des perdreaux de l'année : « C'est vraiment l'enfer »… « Y a de quoi traumatiser un mec »…

C'est souvent là qu'en deuxième division les cartes sont rebattues. Des bateaux de générations antérieures passent devant des plus récents. Ils ont été mieux fiabilisés ou sont conduits par de plus vieux renards ou vieilles renardes. Ici, l'expérience paye !

Je me dis souvent que dans ces mers, la résistance des bateaux révèle la manière de raisonner des skippers et par les choix de navigation s'affirment les personnalités et les émotions. Mais c'est de la psychologie de bistro et le zinc est encore loin. Il y a de la flotte à avaler avant d'y arriver.

Les mers du Sud, c'est une autre dimension. Une fois que tu y as été… je ne vais pas parler de drogue, on n'est pas dépendant, mais c'est rare de ne pas vouloir y retourner.

L'objectif, c'est de passer les mers du Sud en chaussons, sans te mouiller. Tu restes sous la casquette avec les voiles d'avant sur enrouleurs. Tu ne t'exposes que pour envoyer le spi ou le grand gennak. Là-bas, il faut te préserver.

La tactique de l'autruche

Samantha Davies – 2008

RALENTIR, CE N'EST PAS TOUJOURS LA SÉCURITÉ, IL FAUT AVANCER AVEC LES ÉLÉMENTS. SI TU ES TROP LENTE, C'EST COMME MARCHER À RECULONS SUR UN TAPIS ROULANT. TU TE COUPES DU RYTHME NATUREL DES VAGUES ET ÇA AUGMENTE LES TORSIONS. POUR RESTER DANS LE BON SENS, TU DOIS TE FAIRE VIOLENCE.
MAIS SI TU VAS TROP VITE, TU PEUX ATTEINDRE LA CAPACITÉ MAXIMALE DE TENSION D'UNE DES PIÈCES DE TON BATEAU. IL SUFFIT QU'UNE SOIT PLUS FAIBLE QUE LES AUTRES, QUE TU L'AIES MAL CONTRÔLÉE AVANT LE DÉPART, ET TOUT CASSE.
DE TOUTE FAÇON SUR UN TAPIS ROULANT, IL FAUT QUE TU AILLES À SON RYTHME, NI PLUS NI MOINS, SINON ÇA DEVIENT VITE CASSE-GUEULE. ET LES MERS DU SUD, C'EST UN GRAND ET PUISSANT TAPIS ROULANT QUI TOURNE AUTOUR DE LA TERRE.
19 NŒUDS SUR LA DERNIÈRE HEURE. JE PEUX ENCORE APPUYER.
PENDANT LES ENTRAÎNEMENTS, JE M'ÉTAIS ÉTABLI DES MOYENNES DE VITESSES MAXIMALES.
20 NŒUDS. J'APPUIE ENCORE UN PEU
21 NŒUDS. ON VA COMMENCER À FAIRE GAFFE.
ENFERMÉE DANS LE BATEAU, JE FAISAIS L'AUTRUCHE ET NAVIGUAIS EN FONCTION DE CES MOYENNES. LES ATTEINDRE ET NE PAS LES DÉPASSER.
ROXY
C'ÉTAIT MA PREMIÈRE FOIS EN SOLITAIRE DANS CES MERS-LÀ, J'AI ADORÉ.

« LE CHALLENGE SPORTIF DU VENDÉE GLOBE EST HYPER FORT, MAIS, AVANT TOUT ET PAR-DESSUS TOUT, CE QUI ME DICTE LE FAIT D'ALLER EN MER, C'EST LA MER, LA MER ELLE-MÊME. EN COURSE OU NON, PROFESSIONNELLEMENT OU EN LOISIR, SUR UN GROS OU UN PETIT BATEAU, JE VAIS SUR L'EAU DÈS QUE JE LE PEUX PARCE QUE LA MER EST LÀ.
IL Y A CETTE CARICATURE ARCHI ÉCULÉE DU GAMIN SUR LA PLAGE, REGARDANT AU LOIN : "DIS, QU'EST-CE QU'IL Y A APRÈS L'HORIZON ?", ET L'ON DIT QUE C'EST POUR ALLER Y VOIR, QU'UN JOUR DEVENU GRAND, CE GAMIN PRENDRA LA MER. ELLE EST BELLE L'IMAGE, NON ? ÇA FAIT PLEURER DANS LES CHAUMIÈRES, ET AVEC ELLE TU PEUX VENDRE N'IMPORTE QUEL PAQUET DE LESSIVE.
SAUF QUE CE GAMIN EXISTE ! C'EST MOI ! JE SUIS PARTI TRÈS TÔT EN MER, À LA VOILE AVEC MES PARENTS ET JE N'AI JAMAIS CESSÉ DE VOULOIR VOIR CET HORIZON QUI N'EN FINIT PAS D'ÊTRE L'HORIZON. ÊTRE AU CONTACT DE L'ÉLÉMENT NATUREL, C'EST ÇA QUI M'ATTIRE, QUI M'ASPIRE VERS LA MER. JE NE SAIS PAS SI JE M'EN LASSERAI UN JOUR. PEUT-ÊTRE JAMAIS.

ARNAUD BOISSIÈRES
VENDÉE GLOBE 2008 ET 2012

LES VOILES QUI CARESSENT LE VENT. LA COQUE QUI GLISSE DANS L'EAU. ET TOI SUR LE BATEAU QUI ANTICIPES LES MOUVEMENTS AVEC LES JAMBES, LE BASSIN, TOUT LE CORPS QUI DANSE – PLUS OU MOINS GRACIEUSEMENT – ET TU BORDES UN PEU, CHOQUES UN BRIN, TU SENS LES ÉLÉMENTS, TU LES ACCOMPAGNES.
JE RESPECTE ÉNORMÉMENT LA MER ET POUR LUI DIRE MON AMOUR, JE PERPÉTUE LES TRADITIONS. POUR LES TROIS CAPS, LE BONNE-ESPÉRANCE, LE LEEUWIN ET LE HORN, JE PRÉVOIS UNE PETITE BOUTEILLE POUR CHACUN DE LEUR PASSAGE. JE BOIS UNE PETITE GORGÉE, À PEINE, J'EN LAISSE COULER UN PEU SUR LE BATEAU ET LE RESTE, JE L'OFFRE À LA MER. POUR CELA, JE SUIS TRADITIONALISTE. SANS CE RESPECT, JE N'AI PLUS DE RAISON D'ALLER EN MER, QUE CE SOIT POUR LE VENDÉE GLOBE OU POUR N'IMPORTE QUELLE OCCASION, LA MER, L'ÉLÉMENT ET SON HISTOIRE.
ENFANT, J'AI ÉCOUTÉ CES HISTOIRES QUI VENAIENT JUSQU'À NOUS PAR LES ONDES OU PAR LE MESSAGE RAPPORTÉ PAR UN TEL QUI A CROISÉ UNE TELLE DE L'AUTRE CÔTÉ DU MONDE, AU MILIEU D'UN OCÉAN, À TELLES LATITUDE ET LONGITUDE. ALORS VITE, JE REGARDE SUR LES CARTES, "MOI AUSSI UN JOUR J'IRAI." ET À MON TOUR, J'ESSAYE DE RACONTER, DE COMMUNIQUER MON ENTHOUSIASME, D'ÉCRIRE DANS CE JOURNAL, D'INTERVENIR SUR CETTE RADIO, DE RÉPONDRE AUX MESSAGES REÇUS VIA LES RÉSEAUX SOCIAUX. PARLER À QUELQU'UN AU TÉLÉPHONE OU À LA CAMÉRA POUR LE PETIT FILM QUE L'ON VA ENVOYER, ET MÊME SE PARLER À SOI-MÊME – EN MER, JE ME PARLE BEAUCOUP À HAUTE VOIX –, ÇA M'AIDE À CONTINUER, À SUIVRE MA ROUTE. TOUT ÇA, C'EST DU RESPECT À LA MER, POUR LA MER ET CE QU'ELLE NOUS TRANSMET.
ET PRENDRE LE TEMPS DE BIEN REGARDER LA MER, LE VENT, LE BATEAU, POUR POUVOIR LES DÉCRIRE AUX AUTRES, FACTUELLEMENT, ÇA ME PERMET DE CRÉER UN RECUL SUR MES ANALYSES ET DONC SUR MA STRATÉGIE. ÇA M'AIDE À PRENDRE LES BONNES DÉCISIONS ET À ANTICIPER. RESPECTER LES ÉLÉMENTS, C'EST AUSSI BIEN NAVIGUER, NE JAMAIS SE RETROUVER CONTRE EUX. LA MER TU ES AVEC ELLE, C'EST POUR ÇA QUE TU Y VAS. KERSAUSON A CETTE EXPRESSION "LA VOILE DU TEMPS", "AVOIR LA VOILE DU TEMPS", JOURDAIN DIT MÊME QUE C'EST LA PLUS GROSSE MALADIE DES MARINS, CETTE OBSESSION À TOUJOURS CHERCHER CETTE VOILE EN ABSOLUE ADÉQUATION AVEC LE TEMPS ET LES ÉLÉMENTS.
C'EST POUR CELA QUE JE FAIS LE VENDÉE GLOBE, PARCE QU'AVANT TOUT, ÇA SE PASSE EN MER. ET DANS LE SUD, CETTE MER SEMBLE RESPIRER PLUS LIBREMENT, À PLEINS POUMONS. ALORS J'ESSAYE DE L'ACCOMPAGNER, DE RESPIRER EN HARMONIE AVEC ELLE. ET JE NE M'EN LASSE PAS. J'Y RETOURNE, J'Y RETOURNE , J'Y RETOURNE. »

AU SUD DE L'AUSTRALIE, 30 NŒUDS DE VENT MOLLISSANT.

VOUS ÊTES SUR L'AUTOROUTE, PIED AU PLANCHER AU VOLANT D'UNE GROSSE CYLINDRÉE, QUAND SOUDAIN, L'UN DE VOS ESSUIE-GLACES A UN PROBLÈME, IL FAUT LE CHANGER.
VOUS DÉCIDEZ : A DE VOUS ARRÊTER À LA PROCHAINE AIRE, CHANGER L'ESSUIE-GLACE, REPRENDRE LA ROUTE. 5 MINUTES D'ARRÊT.
!!
OU : B BLOQUER LA PÉDALE D'ACCÉLÉRATEUR ENFONCÉE, OUVRIR LA VITRE, VOUS EXTRAIRE DE L'HABITACLE À TRAVERS LA PORTIÈRE. VOUS RETROUVER ACCROUPI SUR LE CAPOT, CHANGER D'UNE MAIN L'ESSUIE-GLACE, EN VOUS AGRIPPANT DE L'AUTRE COMPULSIVEMENT À LA GRILLE DU RADIATEUR. PUIS VOUS RÉINTRODUIRE DANS VOTRE VÉHICULE D'UN MOUVEMENT ACROBATIQUE. VOUS RASSEOIR, FERMER LA FENÊTRE, REPRENDRE LE CONTRÔLE DE VOTRE VÉHICULE.
CRACK !!
CE 18 DÉCEMBRE 2008, J'AI OPTÉ POUR LA SECONDE SOLUTION.

JE ME RAPPELLE OUVRIR LES YEUX, VOIR LE CIEL.
GENERALI
JE SUIS À MOITIÉ DANS L'EAU, À MOITIÉ DANS L'AIR. JE NE SUIS PLUS SUR MON BATEAU.
GENERALI
SUSPENDU DANS MON HARNAIS, MAL AU DOS, LES LOMBAIRES ARQUÉES, ET À LA JAMBE... UNE DOULEUR... JE NE PEUX PAS LA DÉCRIRE.
LE MOUSQUETON QUI ME RETIENT S'EST TORDU SOUS LE CHOC. JE DOIS BATAILLER POUR L'OUVRIR...
AAAAAA
... REVENIR À BORD. JE NE SUIS PLUS ATTACHÉ.

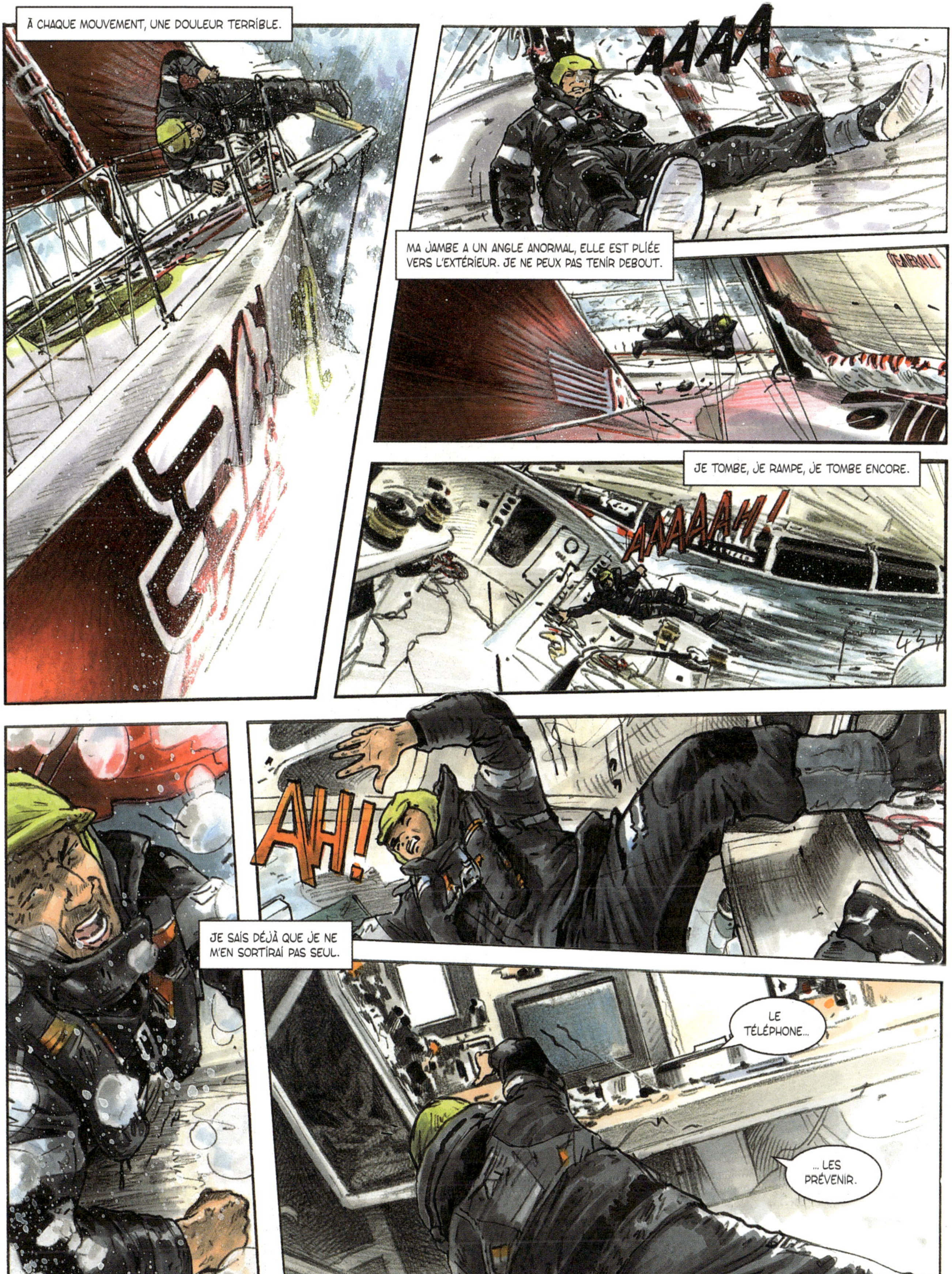
À CHAQUE MOUVEMENT, UNE DOULEUR TERRIBLE.
AAAA
MA JAMBE A UN ANGLE ANORMAL, ELLE EST PLIÉE VERS L'EXTÉRIEUR. JE NE PEUX PAS TENIR DEBOUT.
JE TOMBE, JE RAMPE, JE TOMBE ENCORE.
AAAAAH!
AH!
JE SAIS DÉJÀ QUE JE NE M'EN SORTIRAI PAS SEUL.
LE TÉLÉPHONE...
... LES PRÉVENIR.

YANN, TOUT LE MONDE EST EN ALERTE.
LE MÉDECIN A DIAGNOSTIQUÉ UNE FRACTURE DU FÉMUR ET DE MULTIPLES CONTUSIONS. UNE FRÉGATE QUITTE L'AUSTRALIE ET METTRA DEUX JOURS À ARRIVER, TU ES LOIN DE TOUT MAIS TOUT LE MONDE EST MOBILISÉ.
151
SAFRAN
25
MARC GUILLEMOT S'EST DÉROUTÉ. IL DEVRAIT POUVOIR TOURNER AUTOUR DE TOI DÈS CE SOIR. SAMANTHA DAVIES NAVIGUE AUSSI DANS TA DIRECTION.
EN ATTENDANT, TU VAS DEVOIR TENIR.
MAIS LA DÉCISION – STUPIDE – DE ME RETROUVER À JOUER LES ÉQUILIBRISTES DANS UNE MER CREUSÉE ET AVEC LE BATEAU LANCÉ À PLEINE VITESSE POUR CHANGER UNE PIÈCE À L'AVANT DE MON BOUT-DEHORS...
... N'EST QUE LA CONSÉQUENCE DES MAUVAISES DÉCISIONS QUE J'ENCHAÎNAIS DEPUIS DE TROP LONGUES SEMAINES DÉJÀ.

DANS L'OCÉAN INDIEN, DÈS LES PREMIERS JOURS, NOUS AVONS ÉTÉ CUEILLIS PAR UNE SUITE ININTERROMPUE DE GRAINS, PARFOIS À PLUS DE 60 NŒUDS. ON N'AVAIT AUCUN RÉPIT.
SOUS PILOTE, JE FAIS UN PREMIER DÉPART À L'ABATTÉE. PUIS UN DEUXIÈME, UN TROISIÈME… JE NE COMPRENDS PAS POURQUOI.
DES LATTES CASSENT ET PLEIN DE PETITES CHOSES COMMENCENT À LÂCHER. LE BATEAU SE DÉGRADE. ET À METTRE DES PANSEMENTS ICI ET LÀ, JE M'ÉPUISE, J'EN OUBLIE DE DORMIR.
LA RÉCUPÉRATION EST UN ÉQUILIBRE PRÉCAIRE. MON BUT EST D'ÊTRE ENTRE 50 ET 100 % DE "MA BATTERIE INTERNE". SI JE SUIS EN DESSOUS, JE DOIS M'IMPOSER D'ALLER DORMIR, QUITTE À METTRE LE BATEAU À L'ARRÊT COMPLET.
PLUS D'UNE FOIS PENDANT CETTE PÉRIODE, J'AI ÉTÉ EN DESSOUS DE CETTE LIMITE ET JE NE SUIS PAS ALLÉ DORMIR.
LA RAISON DES DÉCROCHÉS DU PILOTE, LÀ D'OÙ TOUT DÉCOULE TECHNIQUEMENT, JE NE L'AI IDENTIFIÉE QU'APRÈS ÊTRE REVENU À TERRE.
EN S'ÉLOIGNANT DU PÔLE NORD MAGNÉTIQUE, ON A DES INTERFÉRENCES DANS L'ÉLECTRONIQUE DU BORD.
JE CONNAISSAIS LE PROBLÈME, J'AVAIS EMBARQUÉ UN CAPTEUR CAPABLE D'ÉVITER CES ANOMALIES. MAIS JE N'AI JAMAIS EU LA PRÉSENCE D'ESPRIT DE L'ALLUMER.
LA FATIGUE ENTRAÎNE LA FATIGUE ET J'ÉTAIS ÉPUISÉ.

MAIS SI MON ACCIDENT S'EXPLIQUE PAR CES PROBLÈMES DE PILOTE, D'ÉLECTRONIQUE ET SURTOUT D'ÉTAT PHYSIQUE, IL FAUT REVENIR AU 29 NOVEMBRE, 20 JOURS AVANT, POUR COMPRENDRE POURQUOI J'EN SUIS ARRIVÉ LÀ.
YES!
ALLEZ ! ON NE MOLLIT PAS.
CE JOUR-LÀ, JE SUIS PASSÉ PREMIER AU CLASSEMENT.
Y. ELIES
S. JOSSE
1er
2
JE COMMENCE À Y CROIRE, JE PEUX ÊTRE SUR LE PODIUM, SUR LA PLUS HAUTE MARCHE MÊME ! J'EN SUIS CAPABLE.
GENERALI
ET PUIS LE 7 DÉCEMBRE, CEUX QUI SE SONT DÉCALÉS PLUS AU SUD ME PASSENT.
D'UN STATUT DE LEADER JE PASSE À CELUI D'UN MEC QUI PEUT FAIRE ENTRE CINQ ET DIX ET JE NE L'ACCEPTE PAS.
JE N'ARRIVE PAS À CHANGER MON OBJECTIF.
Y. ELIES
5
ALORS, À CHAQUE DESCENTE AU CLASSEMENT, J'ATTAQUE UN PEU PLUS, MAIS PAS À BON ESCIENT. JE ME BATS CONTRE LES AUTRES, CONTRE MON BATEAU, CONTRE L'OCÉAN. JE DEVIENS UN MERCENAIRE. JE DÉSORGANISE MON SOMMEIL, JE NE VOIS PLUS LES PRIORITÉS. JE PERDS COMPLÈTEMENT LE FIL DE LA COURSE ET JE NE LE RETROUVERAI JAMAIS.
FAIT CHIER !
JE CONNAISSAIS LE SUD. J'Y ÉTAIS PASSÉ EN MULTI-COQUES, DES BATEAUX AVEC LESQUELS ON PEUT JOUER AVEC LES DÉPRESSIONS, ALLER PLUS VITE QU'ELLES, SAUTER DE L'UNE À L'AUTRE.
MAIS EN MONOCOQUE C'EST UNE PREMIÈRE ET LES VITESSES QUE L'ON ATTEINT NE PERMETTENT PAS AUTANT DE POSSIBILITÉS. SI TU ES EN RETARD D'UN TRAIN DE DÉPRESSION SUR CEUX DE DEVANT ALORS TU NE PEUX PLUS LES REJOINDRE.

JE ME SENS PRISONNIER DES ÉLÉMENTS. MON ORGUEIL M'AVEUGLE, ME FAIT PERDRE L'OBJECTIF PREMIER QUI EST CELUI DE TERMINER.
LE VENDÉE GLOBE A MIS EN LUMIÈRE MA CONDITION DE PETIT HOMME FACE À LA MER ET AUX ÉLÉMENTS.
QUELQUES JOURS AVANT L'ACCIDENT, J'ENVOYAIS UN MAIL À MON ÉQUIPE.
De : Yann Eliès – skipper : 2008:12:16
À : Erwan Steff – team manager
L'aventure vient depuis quelques jours de se transformer en combat au corps à corps. L'Indien, l'Apache, le Mohican est un valeureux guerrier. Et les pauvres cow-boys que nous sommes ont sous-estimé l'instinct sauvage de cet océan. Nous, les régatiers aux montures flambant neuves et aux pare-chocs chromés, ne faisons plus route en rangs serrés mais en ordre dispersé. Le champ de bataille laisse, à la lumière de l'aube, apparaître des monocoques mutilés et des marins groggy. Cette description de la situation peut vous paraître exagérée, ce matin du 16 décembre, mais à travers les petits coups de fil [aux autres skippers] et au regard de mon propre état et de celui de mon bateau, voilà ce que je ressens ce matin. Vous l'avez bien compris, l'océan Indien est en train de donner ou non son autorisation de passage [...]. Je me suis réveillé ce matin comme après un long cauchemar. Sonné, presque choqué par la violence des coups. Mais l'Indien qui sommeillait en moi vient lui aussi de se réveiller. J'en ai marre de prendre des coups et de subir. À travers cette lettre et en même temps que je cherche mes mots, je sens que la rébellion monte en moi comme un fils peut en vouloir à son père le jour de l'adolescence. [...] Le combat continue, plus pour très longtemps, mais il faut tenir.
LE SAMEDI 20 DÉCEMBRE 2008, LA FRÉGATE ARUNTA, VENUE D'AUSTRALIE, ME REJOINT, M'ÉVACUE, SOULAGE MA DOULEUR, ME SOIGNE, ME SAUVE... LAISSANT MON BATEAU AU GRÉ DES FLOTS. JE N'AI EU EN TÊTE QUE LA COMPÉTITION ET J'EN AI OUBLIÉ LA NAVIGATION, LES ÉLÉMENTS. UN OUBLI ET UN AVEUGLEMENT QUI ONT ÉTÉ À DEUX DOIGTS DE ME COÛTER LA VIE.

Avec notre bateau, on sait aller vite. On sait naviguer avec, on sait comment le pousser, on sait quand changer de voiles, on sait quand border ou choquer, on sait s'adapter à telle ou telle mer, lisse, creuse, cassée. On le sait. En théorie, on le sait absolument. Parce que quand tu es dans les mers du Sud, la théorie s'effiloche devant une réalité toute simple : es-tu capable d'être à la hauteur de ta théorie ?

Les mers du Sud, ce ne sont pas que les mers du Sud, c'est aussi le temps passé pour y parvenir. Tu mets entre trois et quatre semaines depuis les Sables-d'Olonne, et déjà, seul et sans assistance, c'est rare de passer autant de temps en mer. Au Horn, de l'autre côté, tu ajouteras un mois, si ce n'est plus, à cette longue chevauchée. Et ça, au moins en course, c'est unique. Tu as la théorie aux entraînements, la théorie dans ton hangar, la théorie sur la ligne de départ et puis la vérité du terrain. Techniquement, quand tu connais, tu peux anticiper, du moins avoir l'impression d'anticiper. Bon.

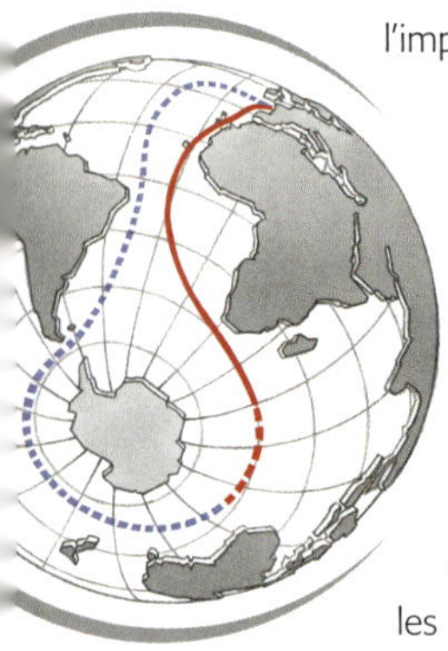

Quand ça va hyper vite et qu'on part au surf, c'est le pied... si ça dure une heure. Si ça dure trois jours tu as peur, du mal à dormir, le stress de péter un truc.

Mais dans les mers du Sud, tu as la théorie, les mathématiques, les coefficients de résistance des matériaux, les moments de redressement, le matériel de rechange, le calcul de l'usure, les alarmes de charges, de pressions, de compressions, de ruptures, mais surtout tu as toi. Tu as toi et même si tu as théorisé aussi sur toi, même si tu t'es entraîné pour être conforme aux théories sur l'humain, sur ta morphologie, sur ta personnalité, même si tu as tout mis en place pour parer à tout te concernant, tu restes toi, un humain si complexe et qui ne peut pas se connaître totalement. Tu ne te connais pas là, dans les mers du Sud. Si tu y es déjà allé, tu vas un peu plus savoir, tu vas être serein parce que tu sais, mais ce que tu sais, c'est qu'au-delà d'une certaine limite, tu ne sais pas. Et savoir qu'on ne sait pas, c'est un bon début pour aller loin. Tu vas aller peut-être plus lentement que ton voisin qui ne sait pas qu'il ne sait pas et qui va sûrement casser puisqu'il ne sait pas, mais qui, s'il ne casse pas, aura de grandes chances d'être devant toi aux Sables-d'Olonne.

Si tu as les compétences, et seulement si tu les as – mais mine de rien beaucoup de gens les ont ces compétences –, la différence sur un Vendée Globe se fera dans l'engagement. Quand tu attaques, dans le Sud, tu fais plus d'un départ au lof par jour. Alors il faut vouloir y aller.

La théorie, pour aller vite surtout quand il y a du vent, c'est d'être à la limite de ton bateau. Au-delà de cette limite, tu as une perte de vitesse, et une usure qui va diminuer à plus ou moins court terme ta performance alors que tu as encore un à deux mois de mer. Et bien sûr, tu as aussi la casse et l'au revoir au Vendée Globe.

Cette limite, tu la connais et tu l'as repérée en entraînement sur l'eau. Mais l'une de tes principales alertes pour ne pas la dépasser, c'est toi, ton ressenti, ton feeling. Dans le Sud, aux vitesses que tu atteins, au vent soutenu qui ne s'arrête jamais, à cette houle puissante et longue, à cette durée qui n'en finit pas, tu ne te connais plus. Tu perds tes repères. Tu n'as plus la sensation de cette limite.

Les bateaux vont de plus en vite et peuvent donc éviter des tempêtes plus facilement. Plus on ira vite, plus on arrivera à jouer avec les systèmes météo. La vitesse est une sécurité dans ces cas-là.

Souvent, tu es en dessous parce que les signaux sont plus loin que là où tu pensais qu'ils étaient. Ce sont les mers du Sud et leur changement d'échelle. Mais si tu te crois plus fort, invincible, et que tu essayes de t'adapter trop rapidement, de reformater en urgence le logiciel de ton cerveau, généralement tu te plantes et tu casses.

Pour retrouver le bon endroit où placer le curseur, tu as deux leviers à mettre en action. La technologie, avec tous ses indicateurs objectifs, va t'aider. Tu restes à l'intérieur, tu débranches tes émotions, tu analyses froidement les chiffres et les voyants que tu as devant toi. Habituellement, tu navigues beaucoup aux sons, les bruits sont très évocateurs de l'état de ton bateau, alors il faut continuer à les écouter, mais à l'inverse de tes habitudes, tu les isoles et tu les interroges séparément pour éviter que le subjectif, la sensation, prenne le dessus. Tu te mets au service de ton bateau et des éléments naturels, tu vas au-delà de l'humain, tu deviens une machine qui accepte, intègre, trie, priorise, conclut, agit, strictement, sans affect.

L'autre levier à actionner, c'est tout de même tes sensations. Parce que si tu ne t'en préoccupes pas, elles vont venir parasiter la machine que tu cherches à devenir, tes calculs seront faussés. Alors il faut t'habituer aux hautes vitesses et aux conditions de ces mers. Y passer et y revenir, en solo, en équipage, en course et en record, plus tu iras, plus tu navigueras à la limite de ton bateau, à sa quintessence. Si tu navigues beaucoup sur des multicoques qui, par essence, vont plus vite que les monocoques, alors arrivé dans le Sud tu seras plus à l'aise, plus serein, ton corps et ton cerveau accepteront de vivre avec la vitesse permanente. Sinon tu as la possibilité de cultiver ta personnalité de tête brûlée, généralement ça marche. Ou ça casse.

La chose la plus dure, c'est de rester à haut régime. En vitesse, un peu, mais surtout en concentration.

Un des marqueurs, c'est d'être toujours à la limite du départ au lof, quand le bateau se couche du côté où il était déjà penché. Tu es à fond, le vent forcit d'un chouïa et ton bateau se couche. Si tu es prêt, ce n'est rien, tu lâches un peu l'écoute, tu diminues la pression subie par ton bateau et il se redresse. Tu re-règles tes voiles et c'est reparti. Le bateau s'est à peine arrêté, il n'en a pas eu le temps, mais c'est un des signes qui te montrent que tu es là où il faut être pour aller vite. Sauf que ça use tes voiles qui viennent frapper l'eau et, à force, perdent de leur performance, et ça t'use aussi car c'est un petit coup de tension qui s'additionne au reste. Donc en amont, à terre, tu dois avoir réfléchi à la gestion de l'usure de ton matériel et à ta propre usure. Tu n'es qu'un humain ! Parfois, mieux vaut lever le pied un temps, se reposer, récupérer et mieux attaquer ensuite. Le Vendée Globe, c'est une course de fond qui se cherche dans le sprint. Tu joues avec le potentiel maximal de ton bateau au quotidien, mais aussi et surtout avec ton potentiel.

Le niveau de concentration et d'engagement que tu as est très étonnant quand tu es dans un cercle vertueux et efficace. Tu es dans un environnement où tu maîtrises, où tu essayes de maîtriser, l'ensemble des paramètres en même temps. À tel point que, par moments, tu as l'impression d'être devenu un robot.

Dans le Grand Sud, le principal facteur sur lequel tu peux jouer, c'est toi.

Pour des raisons de sécurité liées aux glaces échappées de l'Antarctique et aux capacités des différents centres de secours maritimes internationaux, la direction de course du Vendée Globe définit des "portes". Deux points GPS forment les extrémités d'une ligne géographique qu'il faut soit couper en un point, soit laisser entièrement dans son sud. Les bateaux ne peuvent donc descendre trop près de l'Antarctique et de ses icebergs. Ces portes, par leur largeur de plus de 600 km, tentent de ne pas fermer le jeu stratégique, laissant la possibilité d'options météo. La porte et ses deux extrémités ne sont évidemment pas matérialisées au milieu des océans comme lorsque l'on va virer une bouée en régate. La notion de portes relève d'une géographie virtuelle.

* TEMPS UNIVERSEL.

ALLEZ VITE, VITE, VITE !
LA PÉTOLE ARRIVE, IL FAUT SE TIRER D'ICI.
EH! IL Y A PLUS DE VENT QUE PRÉVU!
C'EST BON ÇA !
JE VAIS PASSER SOUS L'ANTICYCLONE SANS MÊME QU'IL ME RALENTISSE.
ET PERSONNE N'A PU ME SUIVRE.
SI ÇA TIENT, J'AURAI 150 MILLES D'AVANCE D'ICI TROIS JOURS.
BANQUE POPULAIRE

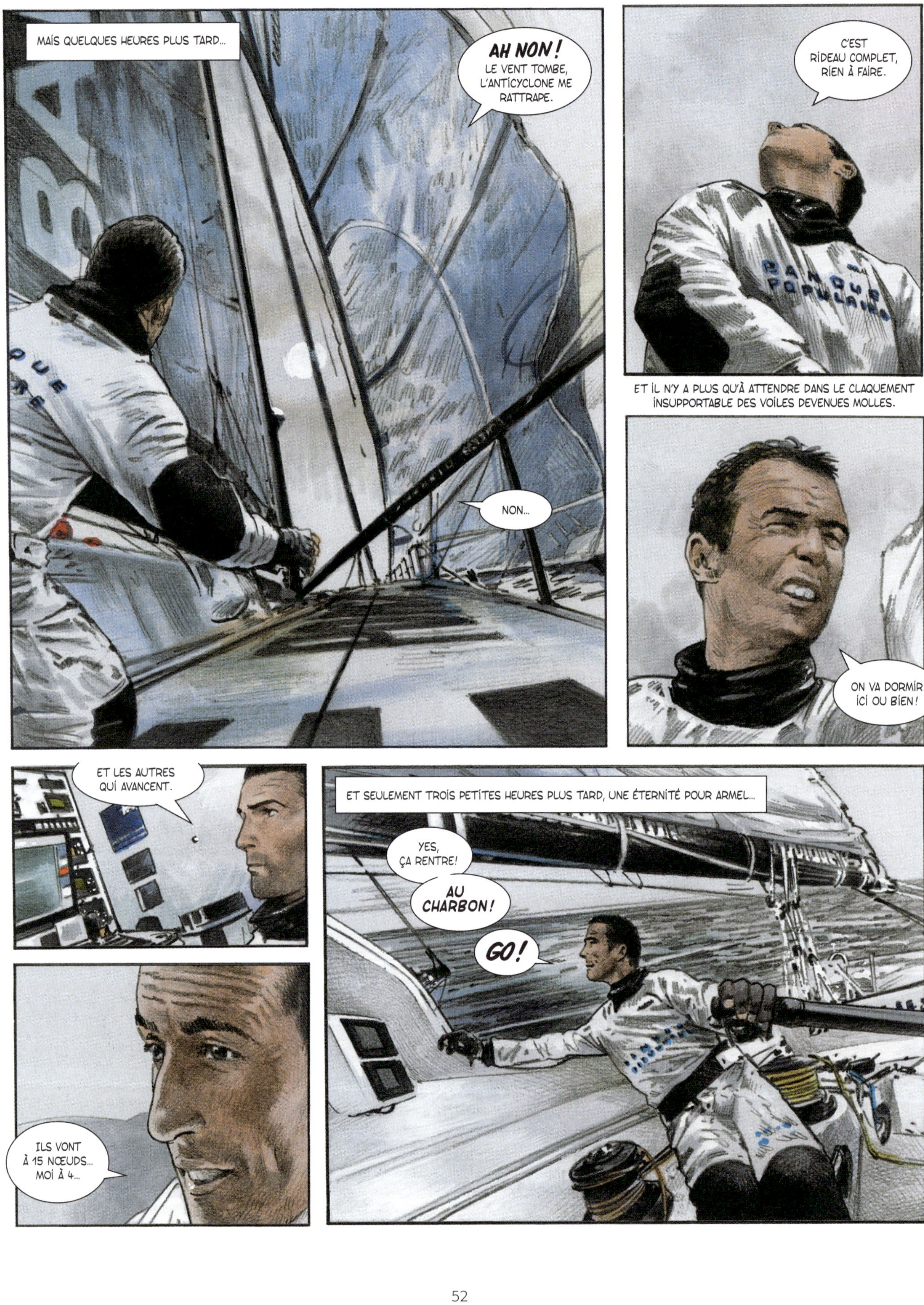
MAIS QUELQUES HEURES PLUS TARD...
AH NON ! LE VENT TOMBE, L'ANTICYCLONE ME RATTRAPE.
NON...
C'EST RIDEAU COMPLET, RIEN À FAIRE.
ET IL N'Y A PLUS QU'À ATTENDRE DANS LE CLAQUEMENT INSUPPORTABLE DES VOILES DEVENUES MOLLES.
ON VA DORMIR ICI OU BIEN !
ET LES AUTRES QUI AVANCENT.
ILS VONT À 15 NŒUDS... MOI À 4...
ET SEULEMENT TROIS PETITES HEURES PLUS TARD, UNE ÉTERNITÉ POUR ARMEL...
YES, ÇA RENTRE !
AU CHARBON !
GO !

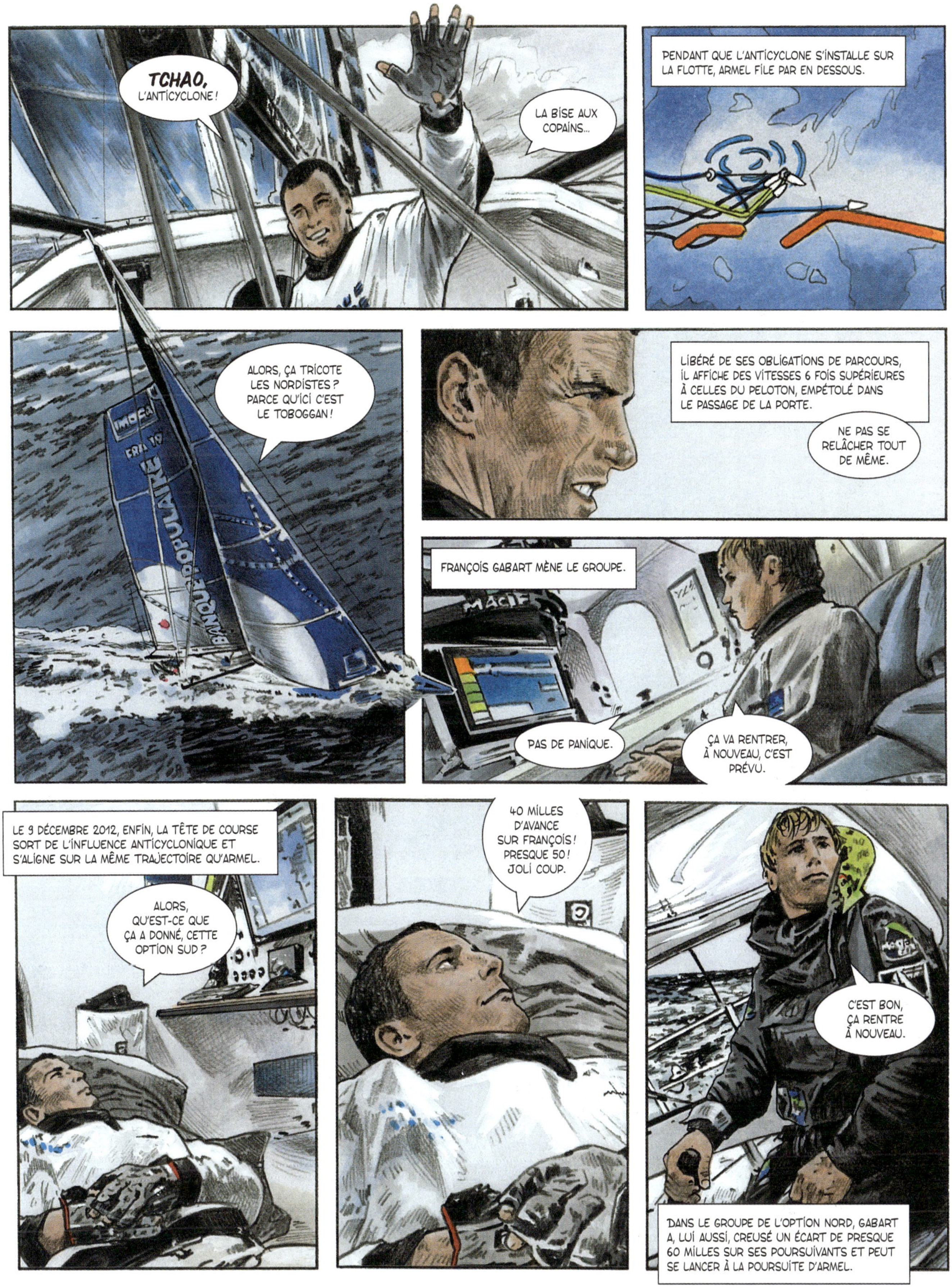
TCHAO, L'ANTICYCLONE !
LA BISE AUX COPAINS...
PENDANT QUE L'ANTICYCLONE S'INSTALLE SUR LA FLOTTE, ARMEL FILE PAR EN DESSOUS.
ALORS, ÇA TRICOTE LES NORDISTES ? PARCE QU'ICI C'EST LE TOBOGGAN !
LIBÉRÉ DE SES OBLIGATIONS DE PARCOURS, IL AFFICHE DES VITESSES 6 FOIS SUPÉRIEURES À CELLES DU PELOTON, EMPÉTOLÉ DANS LE PASSAGE DE LA PORTE.
NE PAS SE RELÂCHER TOUT DE MÊME.
FRANÇOIS GABART MÈNE LE GROUPE.
PAS DE PANIQUE.
ÇA VA RENTRER, À NOUVEAU, C'EST PRÉVU.
LE 9 DÉCEMBRE 2012, ENFIN, LA TÊTE DE COURSE SORT DE L'INFLUENCE ANTICYCLONIQUE ET S'ALIGNE SUR LA MÊME TRAJECTOIRE QU'ARMEL.
ALORS, QU'EST-CE QUE ÇA A DONNÉ, CETTE OPTION SUD ?
40 MILLES D'AVANCE SUR FRANÇOIS ! PRESQUE 50 ! JOLI COUP.
C'EST BON, ÇA RENTRE À NOUVEAU.
DANS LE GROUPE DE L'OPTION NORD, GABART A, LUI AUSSI, CREUSÉ UN ÉCART DE PRESQUE 60 MILLES SUR SES POURSUIVANTS ET PEUT SE LANCER À LA POURSUITE D'ARMEL.

LE VENT ET LA MER S'ALIGNENT ALORS, ET LE CAP SUIVI PAR LES NAVIGATEURS EST PARFAIT POUR ALLONGER LA FOULÉE, ATTEINDRE LES VITESSES MAXIMALES DES BATEAUX.
DURANT TROIS JOURS, MÊME TRAJECTOIRE, MÊME SYSTÈME MÉTÉO, LES CONDITIONS SONT IDYLLIQUES POUR ENQUILLER LES MILLES.
MACIF
MER
À CE PETIT JEU, FRANÇOIS GABART ENCHAÎNE LES RECORDS DE DISTANCES PARCOURUES EN SOLO, EN MONOCOQUE, EN 24 HEURES. À PLUSIEURS REPRISES, IL AFFOLE LES COMPTEURS ET ÉTABLIT UN MAXIMUM DE 545,3 MILLES. SOIT LA VITESSE MOYENNE DE 22,72 NŒUDS ! TROIS DE PLUS QUE LE PRÉCÉDENT RECORD DATANT DE 2003.
ARMEL LE CLÉAC'H NE LÂCHE RIEN, MAINTENANT L'ÉCART AVEC LE PELOTON DE TÊTE.
MAIS IL NE PEUT QUE CONSTATER QU'INEXORABLEMENT, FRANÇOIS GABART SE RAPPROCHE.
LEURS BATEAUX SONT POURTANT QUASI IDENTIQUES, SORTIS DU MÊME MOULE...
... MAIS À TERRE, ILS N'ONT PAS FAIT LES MÊMES CHOIX.

*LE NOMBRE DE VOILES À BORD DES IMOCA EST LIMITÉ. VOIR EXPLICATIONS ET DÉTAILS PAGE 118.

D'où que les vents souffleront…

Vincent Riou

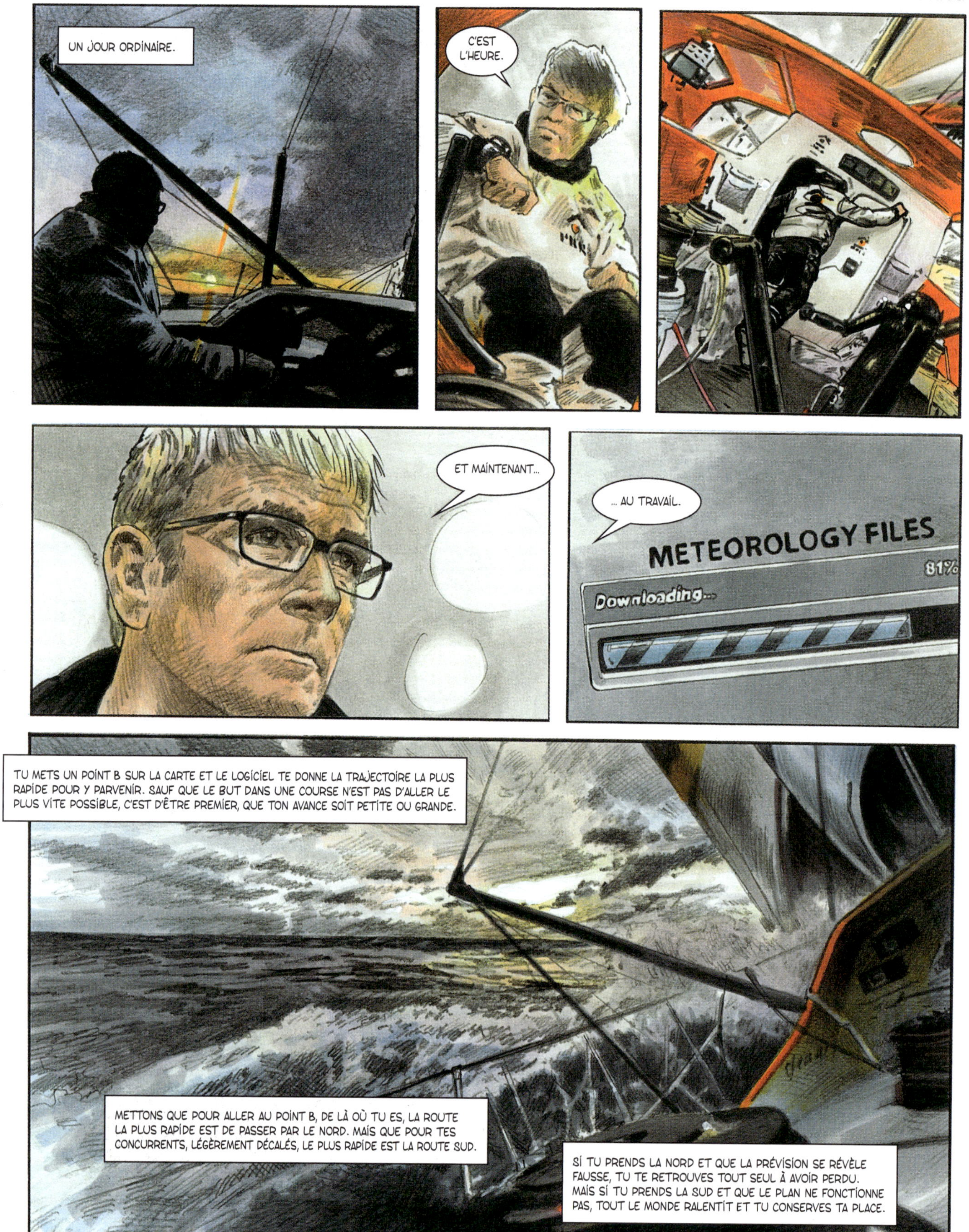

EN FONCTION DE TES AMBITIONS, TU VAS AVOIR DES RAISONS OU NON DE JOUER DES COUPS.
Cap de Bonne-Espérance
Porte Atlantique
Porte Kerguelen
ARMEL LE CLÉAC'H, EN 2012, IL EST LÀ POUR LA PREMIÈRE PLACE, RIEN D'AUTRE, IL A DÉJÀ ÉTÉ DEUXIÈME EN 2008. ALORS JAMAIS IL N'A HÉSITÉ. À LA DESCENTE DE L'ATLANTIQUE, IL PASSE DANS UN TROU D'AIGUILLE ENTRE DEUX BOUTS D'ANTICYCLONE. IL N'Y A QUE THOMSON QUI LE SUIT LÀ-DEDANS.
Cap Leeuwin
Porte Australie Ouest
Îles Kerguelen
Îles Heard
ET DANS L'OCÉAN INDIEN, QUAND UNE GROSSE BULLE SANS VENT ARRIVE POUR SE POSITIONNER SUR LA PORTE, IL RECOMMENCE. IL EST LE SEUL À LA COUPER À L'OUEST. D'UN POINT DE VUE STRATÉGIQUE, ARMEL A EU DES OPTIONS TRÈS ENGAGÉES, ÇA DONNE DU PIMENT, C'EST LA MAGIE DE JOUER AVEC LE VENT ET LES AILES QUE DONNE LA COMPÉTITION.
A
B
A
Δ3h
POUR CES RAISONS, ON NE VA PAS RÉFLÉCHIR EN TERMES DE TRAJECTOIRES MAIS D'ENVELOPPE DE TRAJECTOIRES. ÇA VA NOUS PERMETTRE D'ASSOCIER LA VITESSE PURE AU CONTRÔLE DES ADVERSAIRES. TU PARS DE TON POINT A ET TU METS UN DELTA DE QUELQUES HEURES SUR TON POINT B. TU OBTIENS ALORS UNE ENVELOPPE DE TRAJECTOIRES QUI TE PERMET DE PRENDRE LE PLUS TARDIVEMENT POSSIBLE LA DÉCISION DE QUELLE ROUTE TU VAS SUIVRE ET DONC TE DONNER PLUS DE TEMPS POUR VOIR CE QUE FONT LES AUTRES.
SALUT, TOUT LE MONDE, TOUT VA BIEN À BORD!
PRB
BIEN SÛR, TU FAIS LES ENVELOPPES DE TOUS TES CONCURRENTS DIRECTS POUR POUVOIR ANTICIPER LEURS MANŒUVRES ET LES CONTRÔLER. NORMALEMENT, AVEC LES LOGICIELS ACTUELS, TU SAIS LE FAIRE ET TU SAIS QUE TOUS TES VOISINS SAVENT LE FAIRE AUSSI BIEN QUE TOI. EN TOUT CAS, SI CHACUN ET CHACUNE EST À 100 % DE SES CAPACITÉS INTELLECTUELLES ET PHYSIQUES... ALORS À TOI DE FATIGUER LA CONCURRENCE!
DANS CE DOMAINE, LES TECHNIQUES DE GUERRE PSYCHOLOGIQUE ET D'INTOX ÉVOLUENT SANS CESSE... ET ON GARDE ÇA POUR SOI.
MAIS LÀ OÙ ÇA SE COMPLIQUE, C'EST AU MOMENT DE PLACER TON POINT B SUR TA CARTE. SUR LE VENDÉE GLOBE, LE POINT A, C'EST LES SABLES-D'OLONNE, LE POINT B, C'EST LES SABLES-D'OLONNE... TROIS MOIS PLUS TARD. À 2, 3, 5 JOURS, CE N'EST PAS TRÈS DIFFICILE DE PLACER B. MAIS À PLUS... C'EST À TOI DE L'INVENTER. C'EST DE LA STRATÉGIE GLOBALE ET C'EST UN DES GRANDS ENJEUX DE LA COURSE.
UNE DES CLEFS, C'EST DE REGARDER OÙ NAISSENT LES DÉPRESSIONS QUI NOUS ARRIVENT. SI ELLES VIENNENT D'ARGENTINE, DE L'OUEST DE L'INDIEN OU DU GOLFE DU BENGALE, ELLES N'AURONT PAS LES MÊMES COMPORTEMENTS À LONG TERME. ET IL Y A BEAUCOUP DE FOYERS DE DÉPRESSIONS À OBSERVER.

PENDANT LES ANNÉES PRÉCÉDANT LA COURSE, ON SE CONSTRUIT DES ROAD BOOKS AVEC DES SCHÉMAS DE PROBABILITÉS AFFINÉS ET SECTORIELS. ON PREND EN COMPTE LE MAXIMUM D'INFORMATIONS POUR NE PAS VENIR BUTER CONTRE UN MUR SANS VENT COMME TELS CARAVELLE, FRÉGATE OU CLIPPER D'IL Y A DEUX SIÈCLES PAR EXEMPLE. AVEC CETTE MASSE D'INFORMATIONS, ON PEUT PARIER QUE TELLE DÉPRESSION VA TENIR LONGTEMPS OU S'ESSOUFFLER, NOUS EMMENER TRÈS AU SUD OU RESTER PARALLÈLE AUX LATITUDES.
JE VOUS SALUE, MAGELLAN, DRAKE, BOUGAINVILLE!
MERCI DE NOUS AVOIR MONTRÉ LA VOIE, D'AVOIR DÉFRICHÉ, TENTÉ, AFFRONTÉ L'INCONNU ET PARFOIS... D'Y ÊTRE RESTÉS.
HARDI ! ET TÂCHONS DE NE PAS EN FAIRE AUTANT...
ON NAVIGUE AUX CÔTÉS DE L'HISTOIRE ET SE DESSINE LÀ UNE STRATÉGIE À LONG TERME, AU-DELÀ DES STRICTES PRÉVISIONS MÉTÉO.
POUR REVENIR À NOTRE ÉPOQUE, EN 2000, DESJOYEAUX CHOISIT UNE ROUTE NORD, PLUS LONGUE, LAISSANT YVES PARLIER COUPER AU PLUS COURT PAR LE SUD.
CREVÉ, AVEC LA DÉPRESSION QUI S'ESSOUFFLE ET DEMANDE PLUS DE MANŒUVRES, ON SAIT COMMENT L'HISTOIRE S'EST FINIE : BATEAU EN VRAC, MÂT CASSÉ, PÊCHE À LA LIGNE, ARRIVÉE EN 126 JOURS POUR L'UN, EN 93 POUR L'AUTRE... VICTORIEUX.

LA ROUTE SUD EST GÉNÉRALEMENT LA PLUS ATTIRANTE SI TU REGARDES LES PRÉVISIONS MÉTÉO, MAIS ELLE SE TRANSFORME TROP SOUVENT EN IMPASSE. TU TE FATIGUES, TU FATIGUES LE MATÉRIEL, TU NE PEUX PAS GÉRER, TU SUBIS ET TU ES POUSSÉ À LA FAUTE. PAR LE NORD, IL FAUT ÊTRE UN BON COUREUR DE FOND. LA ROUTE EST PLUS LONGUE, IL NE FAUT JAMAIS SE RELÂCHER ET ÊTRE EN PERMANENCE AU MAXIMUM DU POTENTIEL DE TA MACHINE. MAIS C'EST UNE ROUTE MOINS SOLLICITANTE. TU ES DANS LA GESTION DE TON ÉTAT ET DE CELUI DU BATEAU, TU Y CONTRÔLES PLUS TA COURSE. APRÈS, À CHACUN ET CHACUNE SES POINTS FORTS ET SES FAIBLESSES, IL FAUT LES CONNAÎTRE ET COMPOSER AVEC.

Être seul est un plaisir – pour moi en tout cas. Tout le monde ne recherche pas la même chose en faisant du solo et cela ne doit pas obligatoirement rimer avec solitude. Il y a une mauvaise solitude qui vient lorsqu'être en solitaire est subi. Mais moi, je la recherche, je l'attends.

Lorsque tu pars pour aussi longtemps, tu sais que des mécanismes d'adaptation vont se mettre en place. Des marins vont parler à haute voix, s'adresser à un ou une amie réels ou imaginaires, se parler à soi-même, se créer un double, peut-être fantasmer sur qui est qui, donner de l'importance à elle ou à lui. C'est agréable la solitude, il faut juste ne pas s'y laisser enfermer. Pendant le Vendée Globe, il y a tous ces contacts téléphoniques et ses mails auxquels tu es tenu de répondre. Tu ne peux pourtant pas en vouloir à tes sponsors ou à la course. Tu sais pourquoi et comment tu es là, alors ne râle pas, ce serait trop simple. Ces contacts t'empêchent de t'enfermer dans une solitude mais ils ne t'empêchent pas de t'investir dans la solitude.

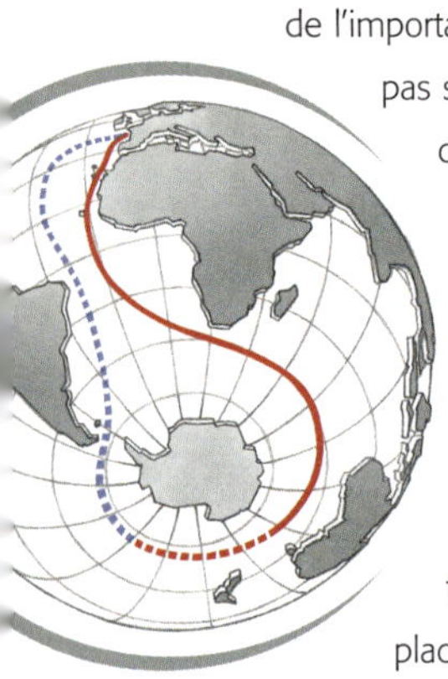

Tu te construis des routines, tu laisses de côté ce qui ne t'est pas important et mettre un quotidien physiquement en place permet également de t'y installer psychologiquement. Tu te libères, tu repousses les questions qui te brouillent le cerveau, tu les reportes à plus tard, quand tu seras revenu à terre, et peut-être auront-elles disparu, tant mieux, elles n'étaient alors que néfastes et inutiles. Ce long passage en solitude me lave, me recentre, range mes idées et ose tirer un trait sur quelques pollutions qui m'accaparent.

La solitude amène le présent, je n'ai que lui à me mettre entre les mains, je ne me disperse pas au gré des sollicitations extérieures. Je suis là, dans mon bateau, dans une quête, une démarche, celle de la course et du Vendée Globe. Vivre le présent et uniquement le présent, c'est un luxe rare aujourd'hui. J'y suis obligé par la course, pour réussir la course, car il me faut rester concentré sur chaque instant, mais je suis aussi un professionnel et cette course s'inscrit dans un parcours global que j'ai en tête. De retour aux Sables-d'Olonne, ma carrière va continuer, mes sponsors vont faire le point, tout cela, j'y pense avant et pendant la course. Mais c'est par la solitude que j'arrive à expulser ces questions. La course, l'enjeu sportif me réclament d'être dans le présent, et paradoxalement c'est la solitude qui me permet d'y accéder pleinement.

Bien sûr, cette solitude doit se gérer. Socialement, les ponts construits entre ma vie et celles de mon entourage peuvent se distendre. Je me charge en expériences rares et exceptionnelles et surtout, en expériences uniques et vécues seul. Il peut être alors dur de les partager. Il ne faut pas que la solitude en mer se traduise, une fois revenu à terre, par un isolement social et affectif. Si je me suis éloigné de mon quotidien terrien et de celui de mes proches, il faut m'y réinvestir, vite !, une fois rentré. Aimer à nouveau toutes ces choses petites ou grandes, m'en émerveiller, m'y plaire et m'en refaire complice.

Dans le Sud, si tu as un pépin, c'est aux autres concurrents de venir te chercher. Donc si tu continues avec un truc techniquement un peu scabreux, tu peux mettre tout le monde dans la mouise. Tu es obligé d'y penser.

Être en solitaire, investi d'une solitude ou non, lorsque l'on fait le tour du monde par les trois caps, cela signifie également un éloignement physique de toute terre habitée. C'est une évidence, mais finalement, c'est rare dans une vie d'humain. Bien sûr, il y a les autres skippers et skippeuses, mais je ne les compte pas, ils sont dans la même instabilité que moi, dans la même expérience, dans la même fragilité. Ils font partie de cet éloignement, de ce vécu qui sort de l'ordinaire et est difficilement dicible, difficilement partageable. Il m'est arrivé, au milieu de l'océan Indien ou du Pacifique, de calculer à combien de kilomètres était le premier point de civilisation. Et lorsque les centaines s'accumulent, lorsque les milliers apparaissent, cela donne un sentiment étrange. Ces calculs m'ont fait du bien, m'ont rasséréné, relaxé, apaisé, je suis venu chercher cette solitude. Je ne sais pas comment j'aurais réagi si j'étais en train de la subir.

Avec l'éloignement, bien entendu, arrivent des questions sur la sécurité. Sur la capacité à compter sur les autres en cas d'accident. Cela change notre manière de percevoir les enjeux, la portée de nos décisions et de nos actes. Mais les actes en eux-mêmes ne changent pas. Bien sûr, il fait souvent froid, bien sûr après un ou deux mois de mer, en course qui plus

Il y a des gens qui comprennent ce que l'on raconte quand on est en mer. Mais la plupart du temps ce n'est qu'entre skippers que l'on peut vraiment s'entendre. On n'a pas besoin d'expliquer nos galères, on sait ce qu'on vit.

est, la fraîcheur physique n'est plus au rendez-vous – bien que souvent compensée par l'expérience acquise au fil des océans parcourus –, bien sûr on objectera tout un tas de facteurs pour expliquer que tout est plus dur dans le Sud. Mais non, les manœuvres sont identiques, ce n'est que la perception que l'on en a qui change et elle est intimement liée à l'éloignement. Faire un virement de bord, un empannage ou changer une voile n'est pas plus dangereux, en soi, dans le Grand Sud qu'en baie des Sables-d'Olonne. L'opération est la même, les enchaînements identiques. Il y a la vitesse qui change, certes, mais la vitesse on a appris à la maîtriser et, physiquement, on s'y est préparé. Par contre, si je me plante, les conséquences seront beaucoup, beaucoup plus compliquées. Si cela tourne mal, je ne pourrai peut-être pas "me rattraper". On n'a qu'une cartouche dans le Grand Sud. Alors si je me plante, si je me plante, si… mais pourquoi me planterais-je ?

À l'approche de Noël, j'étais au sud de la Nouvelle-Zélande. Géographiquement, si tu fais un trou dans le sol, là, en étant en France, tu arrives pas loin d'où j'étais. Ça veut dire que physiquement parlant, tu ne peux pas être plus loin de tes proches sur la planète. Tu viens de traverser l'océan Indien qui est immense, plus de 9 000 km parcourus, et tu t'apprêtes à entrer dans le Pacifique pour 7 000 km jusqu'au Horn. Tu vas te trouver le plus éloigné du moindre humain que tu n'as jamais été – sans parler de tes concurrents bien sûr, mais eux sont avec toi, dans la même précarité, dans le même monde que toi, alors c'est autre chose. Tu es loin de tout et tu sais que la suite va être un éloignement encore plus prononcé parce qu'au milieu du Pacifique, si tu as un problème, tu sais qu'il n'y aura pas d'hélico pour venir te chercher et qu'aucun navire de commerce ne passe par là. Tu es hyper loin, tu le sais et tu es comme devant une porte dont il te faut franchir le seuil.
À ce moment, ma problématique, c'est le bateau et uniquement lui. Je suis plus ou moins au milieu de ma course et je sais que c'est là qu'il ne faut pas flancher, ne rien lâcher. Je suis hyper concentré et à terre, la seule préoccupation… **c'est Noël !** Dès que tu as un journaliste, tu te rends compte que c'est le seul sujet de conversation possible. Je veux rester concentré, penser à mon bateau, je le dis aux journalistes, j'en parle et ils ne peuvent pas s'en empêcher, ils bouclent : "Oui, oui d'accord, mais Noël ?"
Et là, je me suis senti… C'était au-delà de l'éloignement géographique. Je me suis retrouvé encore plus loin qu'il n'est possible de l'être sur notre planète.
J'en avais rien à foutre de Noël, vous ne pouvez pas imaginer à quel point j'en avais rien à foutre. Même le téléphone qui crée un lien avec la terre devenait facteur d'éloignement. Et c'est à ce moment-là que je me suis dit que j'étais tout seul. Vraiment seul.
Mentalement, c'était une période difficile. Peut-être la plus difficile de mon Vendée Globe.

* LISTE "À FAIRE".

LA CONCENTRATION S'ÉMOUSSE...
LES PENSÉES S'ENVOLENT ET UNE FORME DE NONCHALANCE S'INSTALLE.
DIMANCHE.
« JE POURRAIS ME TROUVER DES DIZAINES D'EXCUSES PLUS OU MOINS VALABLES. »
« MAIS IL N'Y EN A QU'UNE DE RÉELLEMENT SINCÈRE : JE N'AVAIS PLUS ENVIE. »
LUNDI.
MARDI.
MERCREDI.
« JE N'AVAIS PLUS L'ENVIE. »

JEUDI.
SCHLACK!!!
ÇA Y EST, LE BOULON A FINI DE SE DÉVISSER, L'AXE A SAUTÉ ET TOUT S'EST ARRACHÉ.
?
LE SAFRAN SE FAIT LA MALLE !
NON ! NON !

AAAAHH !
« EN QUELQUES INSTANTS, JE SUIS GELÉ. »
ABATTRE. **AH, NON !** PLUTÔT LOFER.
NON...
« JE COMMENCE DÉJÀ À FATIGUER. »
NOOON !!
« TENIR UNE PÂLE DE SAFRAN SOUS LA PRESSION DE L'EAU...
AAAHH
... TU LE FAIS UNE FOIS PAS DEUX. »

VITE ! JE NE SAIS PAS QUOI FAIRE MAIS IL FAUT QUE JE LE FASSE !
J'ATTRAPE TOUS LES BOUTS À MA PORTÉE.
JE CHANGE DE CAP, SANS TROP DE RAISON… QUELQUES DEGRÉS.
ET LE BATEAU PART EN MARCHE ARRIÈRE.
JE NE VOIS PLUS RIEN, LE SAFRAN EST PASSÉ SOUS LA COQUE !
SANS LUI, LE BATEAU EST INGOUVERNABLE. SI JE NE TROUVE PAS DE SOLUTION, JE DEVRAI ABANDONNER !
SOUDAIN, DE L'ARRIÈRE, DE GRANDS BRUITS DE CARBONE QUI SE COMPRESSENT ET SE CASSENT !
JE ME PRÉCIPITE.
MAIS ?!
?!
LE SAFRAN S'EST REMIS EN PLACE. TOUT SEUL !
JE FONCE !
KLONG !

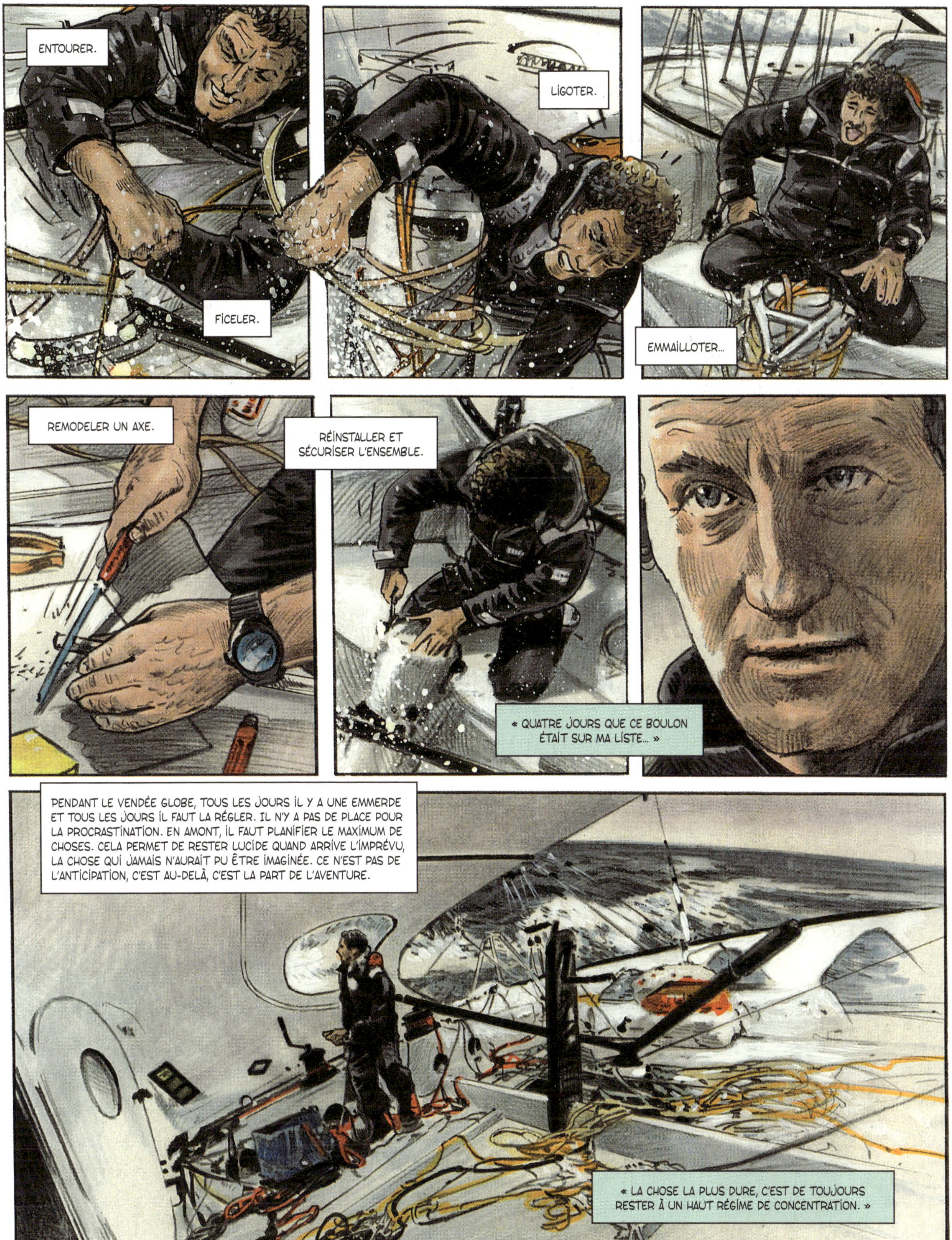
ENTOURER.
FICELER.
LIGOTER.
EMMAILLOTER...
REMODELER UN AXE.
RÉINSTALLER ET SÉCURISER L'ENSEMBLE.
« QUATRE JOURS QUE CE BOULON ÉTAIT SUR MA LISTE... »
PENDANT LE VENDÉE GLOBE, TOUS LES JOURS IL Y A UNE EMMERDE ET TOUS LES JOURS IL FAUT LA RÉGLER. IL N'Y A PAS DE PLACE POUR LA PROCRASTINATION. EN AMONT, IL FAUT PLANIFIER LE MAXIMUM DE CHOSES. CELA PERMET DE RESTER LUCIDE QUAND ARRIVE L'IMPRÉVU, LA CHOSE QUI JAMAIS N'AURAIT PU ÊTRE IMAGINÉE. CE N'EST PAS DE L'ANTICIPATION, C'EST AU-DELÀ, C'EST LA PART DE L'AVENTURE.
« LA CHOSE LA PLUS DURE, C'EST DE TOUJOURS RESTER À UN HAUT RÉGIME DE CONCENTRATION. »

C'EST L'HEURE, DES POSITIONS.
ALORS, JAVIER SANSÓ EST LÀ, DOMINIQUE WAVRE ICI, MIKE GOLDING ET JEAN LE CAM...

JAVIER C'EST POSSIBLE DE L'AVOIR, MÊME AVEC SON BATEAU PLUS RÉCENT QUE LE MIEN. WAVRE ? PEUT-ÊTRE. MAIS ALORS JE RATTRAPE GOLDING AUSSI. LE CAM ? NON, IL EST UN PEU TROP LOIN TOUT DE MÊME. MAIS JAVIER, WAVRE ET MIKE, C'EST POSSIBLE.
LA MÉTÉO, ÇA DIT QUOI ?

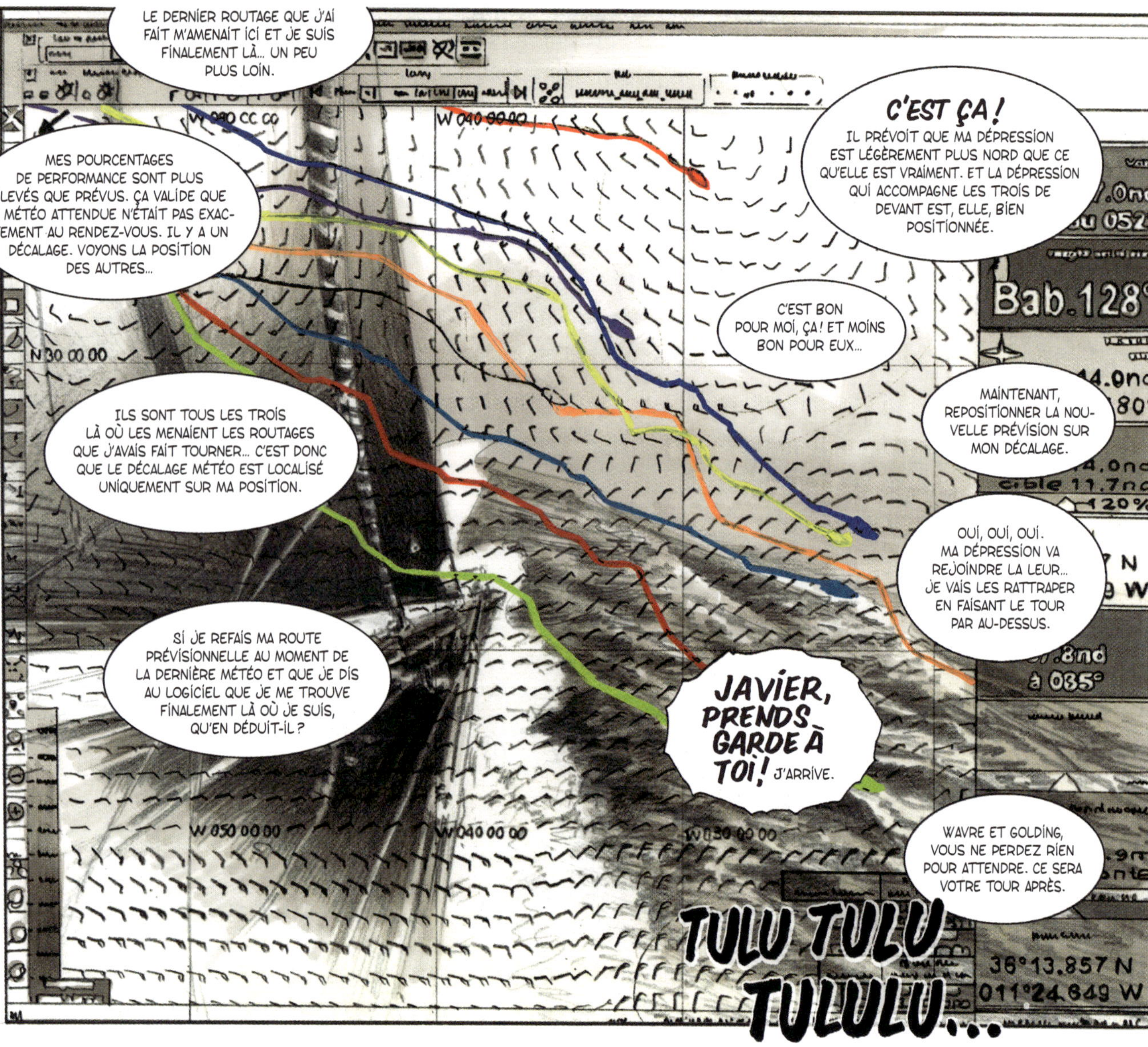
LE DERNIER ROUTAGE QUE J'AI FAIT M'AMENAIT ICI ET JE SUIS FINALEMENT LÀ... UN PEU PLUS LOIN.
MES POURCENTAGES DE PERFORMANCE SONT PLUS ÉLEVÉS QUE PRÉVUS. ÇA VALIDE QUE LA MÉTÉO ATTENDUE N'ÉTAIT PAS EXACTEMENT AU RENDEZ-VOUS. IL Y A UN DÉCALAGE. VOYONS LA POSITION DES AUTRES...
ILS SONT TOUS LES TROIS LÀ OÙ LES MENAIENT LES ROUTAGES QUE J'AVAIS FAIT TOURNER... C'EST DONC QUE LE DÉCALAGE MÉTÉO EST LOCALISÉ UNIQUEMENT SUR MA POSITION.
SI JE REFAIS MA ROUTE PRÉVISIONNELLE AU MOMENT DE LA DERNIÈRE MÉTÉO ET QUE JE DIS AU LOGICIEL QUE JE ME TROUVE FINALEMENT LÀ OÙ JE SUIS, QU'EN DÉDUIT-IL ?
C'EST ÇA ! IL PRÉVOIT QUE MA DÉPRESSION EST LÉGÈREMENT PLUS NORD QUE CE QU'ELLE EST VRAIMENT. ET LA DÉPRESSION QUI ACCOMPAGNE LES TROIS DE DEVANT EST, ELLE, BIEN POSITIONNÉE.
C'EST BON POUR MOI, ÇA ! ET MOINS BON POUR EUX...
MAINTENANT, REPOSITIONNER LA NOUVELLE PRÉVISION SUR MON DÉCALAGE.
OUI, OUI, OUI. MA DÉPRESSION VA REJOINDRE LA LEUR... JE VAIS LES RATTRAPER EN FAISANT LE TOUR PAR AU-DESSUS.
JAVIER, PRENDS GARDE À TOI ! J'ARRIVE.
WAVRE ET GOLDING, VOUS NE PERDEZ RIEN POUR ATTENDRE. CE SERA VOTRE TOUR APRÈS.
TULU TULU TULULU...
Bab.128°
36°13.857 N
011°24.649 W

ALLÔ, ARNAUD, ICI LE PC COURSE. ON T'A PRÉVU POUR PASSER À LA VACATION-MÉDIA TOUT À L'HEURE. ÇA SERAIT BON POUR TOI ?
OK, VOUS M'APPELEZ À L'HEURE DITE, JE TENDS L'OREILLE.
REVENONS À NOS BATEAUX. LE DÉCALAGE DE MA DÉPRESSION VA IMPACTER LA LEUR D'ICI ENVIRON SIX HEURES.
DONC EUX AUSSI NE VONT PAS ÊTRE LÀ OÙ LA MÉTÉO LES PRÉVOIT. MOUAIIIS...
JAVIER SE RETROUVERAIT ICI.
WAVRE ET GOLDING SERAIENT LÀ.
UN PEU PLUS BORDÉ, C'EST MIEUX.
... SI JE REFAIS LA TRAJECTOIRE DE JAVIER MAIS AVEC 10° D'ANGLE DE VENT EN MOINS...
J'ABATS UN PETIT PEU.
... ET POUR LE RATTRAPER... SI J'ENVOIE EN VOILE D'AVANT LE J1, JE GAGNE 1,2 NŒUD PENDANT 2H MAIS JE PERDS 10 MINUTES À CHAQUE MANŒUVRE. ET APRÈS IL FAUDRA RENVOYER LE J2 PARCE QUE LE VENT VA FORCIR. ANTICIPER ET PRÉPARER LE CHANGEMENT DE VOILE, C'EST 30 MINUTES D'EFFORT. ET EN PLEIN MILIEU JE VAIS DEVOIR PASSER À LA RADIO. **MERDE !** ÇA S'ENCHAÎNE MAL, C'EST LE BORDEL, LÀ.
BON, JE RAPPELLE LE PC COURSE POUR LEUR DIRE QUE FINALEMENT JE SUIS OCCUPÉ. C'EST LE SPONSOR QUI VA RÂLER... QUOIQUE CE SOIT QUAND MÊME BIEN DE PASSER À LA RADIO...
JE VAIS PLUTÔT CHANGER MES PLANS.
JE GARDE LE J2 MÊME SI CE N'EST PAS EXACTEMENT LA VOILE DU TEMPS, MAIS JE RESTE DEHORS, LA MAIN SUR LES ÉCOUTES POUR ÊTRE AU MAXIMUM DU BATEAU SOUS CETTE CONFIGURATION.
TOUT À L'HEURE, APRÈS LA RADIO, LE JOUR VA TOMBER ET JUSTE AVANT, JE DEVRAIS POUVOIR ENVOYER LE J1. LA NUIT IL N'Y A PAS DE CLASSEMENT, MA POSITION NE DONNERA DONC PAS L'INFORMATION DU DÉCALAGE MÉTÉO AUX TROIS AUTRES.
ET À PARTIR DE LÀ, MÊME POUR UNE HEURE DE BÉNÉFICE, JE FAIS LA MANŒUVRE. CROQUER JAVIER, ÇA FAIT UNE BELLE MOTIVATION.

ON VA DÉJÀ POSITIONNER LA VOILE EN PIED DE MÂT. ÇA SERA ÇA DE FAIT.
ILS SONT GENTILS À TERRE : "NOS NOUVELLES VOILES ONT GAGNÉ EN LÉGÈRETÉ, 50 KG !" TU PARLES ! C'EST 50 KG À SEC, MAIS LÀ ELLES SONT TREMPÉES. ET ÇA FAIT COMBIEN 50 KG TREMPÉS ? HEIN ?
ALLEZ LA MULE TAIS-TOI ET TIRE !!
HÉ !
PFUUU... SONNÉ. JE VAIS ENCORE AVOIR UNE BELLE BOSSE, UNE DE PLUS. C'EST LE MÉTIER QUI RENTRE. EN AVANT !

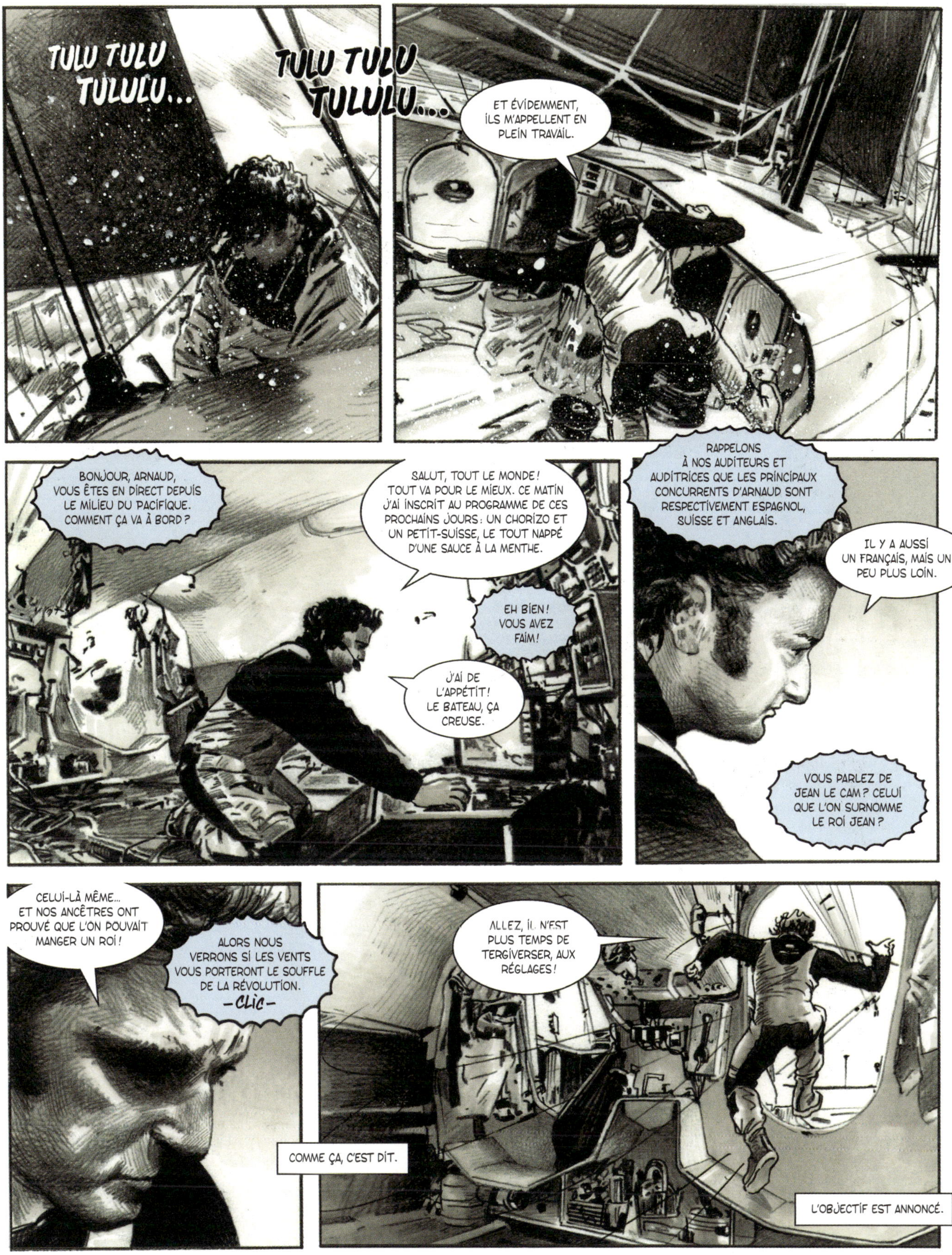
TULU TULU TULULU...
TULU TULU TULULU...
ET ÉVIDEMMENT, ILS M'APPELLENT EN PLEIN TRAVAIL.
BONJOUR, ARNAUD, VOUS ÊTES EN DIRECT DEPUIS LE MILIEU DU PACIFIQUE. COMMENT ÇA VA À BORD ?
SALUT, TOUT LE MONDE ! TOUT VA POUR LE MIEUX. CE MATIN J'AI INSCRIT AU PROGRAMME DE CES PROCHAINS JOURS : UN CHORIZO ET UN PETIT-SUISSE, LE TOUT NAPPÉ D'UNE SAUCE À LA MENTHE.
EH BIEN ! VOUS AVEZ FAIM !
J'AI DE L'APPÉTIT ! LE BATEAU, ÇA CREUSE.
RAPPELONS À NOS AUDITEURS ET AUDITRICES QUE LES PRINCIPAUX CONCURRENTS D'ARNAUD SONT RESPECTIVEMENT ESPAGNOL, SUISSE ET ANGLAIS.
IL Y A AUSSI UN FRANÇAIS, MAIS UN PEU PLUS LOIN.
VOUS PARLEZ DE JEAN LE CAM ? CELUI QUE L'ON SURNOMME LE ROI JEAN ?
CELUI-LÀ MÊME... ET NOS ANCÊTRES ONT PROUVÉ QUE L'ON POUVAIT MANGER UN ROI !
ALORS NOUS VERRONS SI LES VENTS VOUS PORTERONT LE SOUFFLE DE LA RÉVOLUTION.
-CLIC-
COMME ÇA, C'EST DIT.
ALLEZ, IL N'EST PLUS TEMPS DE TERGIVERSER, AUX RÉGLAGES !
L'OBJECTIF EST ANNONCÉ.

18 JOURS PLUS TARD, PENDANT LESQUELS, SANS RELÂCHE, À USER LES PRÉVISIONS MÉTÉO, À BORDER, CHOQUER, CHANGER LES VOILES, FAIRE SUER LES ÉCRANS...
IL EN EST OÙ, LE JAVIER ?
OH!
JE NE LE VOIS PAS. POURTANT...
LÀ !

OUH OUH! JAVIER JE SUIS LÀ! OUH OUH!
P'TAIN, P'TAIN, P'TAIN, ET À 200 MILLES DU CAP HORN.
PAS MOYEN QU'IL ME REPASSE!
LE HORN, JE LE PASSE DEVANT. ET MÊME S'IL N'Y A PAS DE POINTAGE LÀ-BAS, QUE JE FINISSE AUX SABLES DEVANT LUI OU PAS, J'M'EN FOUS, JE VEUX QUE MON CAILLOU AIT LE GOÛT DE CHORIZO.
AH! L'HEURE DES FICHIERS. WAVRE, GOLDING ET LE CAM EN SONT OÙ?
MOUAIIIS... CE NE SERA PAS AVANT LE HORN QUE JE LES RATTRAPERAI. MAIS JAVIER EST TOUJOURS DERRIÈRE. ON ENVOIE LE CHARBON!
VINGT-QUATRE HEURES APRÈS, LE CAP HORN EST LÀ, MAJESTUEUX, ET JAVIER N'EST PAS REPASSÉ DEVANT. QUELQUE TEMPS APRÈS, ARNAUD LUI CÉDERA TOUT DE MÊME SA PLACE... POUR LA REPRENDRE QUELQUES MILLES PLUS LOIN. LES DEUX JOUERONT AU CHAT ET À LA SOURIS JUSQU'À CE QUE JAVIER PERDE SA QUILLE 12 JOURS PLUS TARD. ARNAUD EST ALORS À 100 MILLES DEVANT ET EST PRÊT À REBROUSSER CHEMIN POUR ALLER LUI PORTER ASSISTANCE. MAIS LE PC COURSE L'INFORME QU'UN HÉLICO A PU DÉCOLLER DES AÇORES ET SERA RAPIDEMENT SUR PLACE. LA CHASSE AUX DOMINIQUE WAVRE, MIKE GOLDING ET JEAN LE CAM SE POURSUIVRA, QUANT À ELLE, JUSQU'À LA LIGNE D'ARRIVÉE, MAIS SANS SUCCÈS CETTE FOIS.

Je regarde l'eau. Je commence toujours par regarder l'eau. Ensuite seulement je lève la tête et j'observe le ciel. C'est un rituel immuable, suivre l'ordre c'est comme sortir d'un cocon. Pourtant, je n'ai pas besoin de regarder l'eau. À l'intérieur du bateau, allongé, mon dos tressaute aux coups contre la coque, à genoux, pointes des pieds, cuisses, fesses jouent pour compenser la gîte, debout, mon corps danse, jambes et mains sautent d'une prise à l'autre. Tout me dit la mer et son état, je n'ai pas besoin de la regarder pour la voir. Et pourtant, c'est toujours par elle que je commence en sortant.

Une fois au large, elle est toujours la même et reste immuable tout autour du monde. Réconfortante monotonie. Elle me donne droit à l'évasion, suivre mes pensées, il n'y a que moi qui décide où je vais et ne vais pas. Et pourtant ce n'est qu'une liberté d'émotions, car le corps et le bateau ont accepté un jeu, celui de la course, qui impose direction, manœuvre, planning, affrontement avec les calmes et les tempêtes. Mais regarder cette eau m'ouvre à toutes les libertés. Plonger dans son propre inconnu, dans son infini, dans sa personnalité, la laisser s'exprimer sans peur de la direction qu'elle prend, l'eau libère par sa régularité et son unicité.

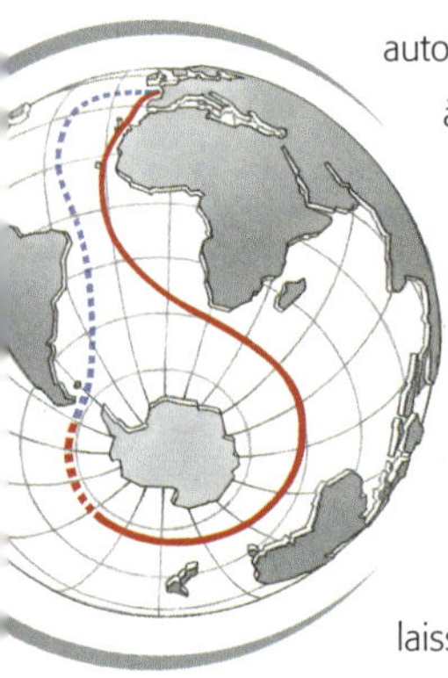

La regarder c'est ce qui, paradoxalement, me lie le plus à ma vie de Terrien, ma vie sociale. En contemplation, je navigue dans ce que je suis et ce qui fait que je le suis. Mon copain, ma copine, les enfants, les potes, potesses, soirées à boire des coups, à parler de tout et de rien, l'appartement, la maison, les prêts à rembourser et le loyer, je survole mon quotidien, ouvre des portes, regarde sous un autre angle.

Et alors je prends des résolutions : manger sainement, n'être plus que bio et éthique, plus attentif à mes proches, écouter avant de parler... et de retour à terre, je recommence comme avant car je n'aurai plus le temps de regarder l'eau. Je suis qui je suis, il n'y a pas de tour de magie !

L'eau est toujours la même quel que soit ce que tu es au moment de la contempler, un miroir. C'est dur de s'y regarder, mais tellement fascinant. Il faut dépasser son premier ego et enfin plus besoin de se cacher, être à poil de l'intérieur. Et rien n'est grave car tu sais, rassurant, que tu reviendras au port. Mais en mer pour longtemps, tu as l'espace pour déposer tes petites hontes.

Assis dans le cockpit, je regarde l'eau et me vois flottant au-dessus, très proche de la surface, jouant parallèle aux vagues qui montent, descendent, tournent, pics et arrondis, un albatros planant pendant plusieurs minutes, de longues minutes. Je dissocie mon physique de mon intellect, et je me regarde. C'est bon de pouvoir s'assumer, Narcisse. Ça fait grandir, on se voit comme on est, tout simplement petit.

Bien sûr, l'eau n'est jamais la même. On y traque les variations, extase devant le camaïeu de bleus, verts, gris, noirs. On se noie en suivant ses évolutions, ses tourbillons, son agitation et ça nous calme, on vogue dessus. N'être que strict spectateur – pour un temps car après il faudra reprendre les commandes de la progression –, quel confort pour le corps ! Je souris à je ne sais quoi, je parle à cette couleur et à ce mouvement, j'y crache voir ce qu'elle en fera, disparition, aucun impact, je m'y abandonne. Je regarde la mer, n'importe quand et si vient la pluie, alors je l'admire aussi. C'est immense la pluie, presque autant que la mer, peut-être même plus que la mer.

Regarder le ciel ne vient qu'après la mer. Je peux même ne pas prendre le temps de regarder le ciel, l'oublier. À quoi bon, la mer me le dit, il s'y reflète et la colore. Je l'ai vu sans le regarder, je l'ai vu depuis mon poste de contrôle et ses écrans.

Dans le Sud, on est décalé en permanence parce qu'on va vite et les longitudes sont rapprochées. Quasiment chaque jour, le soleil se lève une heure plus tôt.

Je regarde le ciel après la mer, mais parfois, je ne peux parvenir à le contempler, je suis en course, au boulot, je le lis et l'analyse. Alors j'attrape un oiseau, un albatros, et c'est lui que je suis, il me masque le ciel. Il me dit son état, sa facilité, sa bonhomie, son énervement, son électricité. L'eau n'a pas d'état d'âme et ne fait que réagir aux choses extérieures tandis que le ciel est changeant, réactif, colérique ou paresseux. Il dicte et ne se laisse pas mener. Il se veut maître mais n'a que la mer à gouverner, impossible ! alors trop heureux lorsqu'il t'y trouve il veut t'imposer ses desideratas, à toi d'en jouer.

Le Grand Sud, c'est la mer, le ciel et encore plus. Le Grand Sud, c'est un ensemble où tu peux perdre tes repères les plus primaires. Quand fait-il jour ou nuit ? Qu'appelle-t-on beau ou mauvais temps ? Le jeu n'est plus de savoir si tu vois le soleil ou si le ciel te paraît bleu, mais plutôt quel est le niveau de luminosité du gris. Agressif ou doux, et son opacité, jusqu'à quelle distance distingue-t-on les choses ? Les choses ? Mais il n'y a rien à distinguer si ce n'est la mer. Tu es le seul bateau, la seule chose dont tu puisses juger de la taille à des centaines de kilomètres à la ronde. As-tu déjà essayé de juger une distance en regardant une vague ? Et une vague d'un océan, d'un que tu ne connais pas ?

Parfois tu te demandes si c'est le jour ou la nuit… c'est toujours gris.

Lors de la descente de l'Atlantique, en quelques heures la température de l'eau chute brutalement, le vent accélère et les affaires chaudes sortent des sacs. Et pourtant ici c'est l'été, une autre idée de l'été. Devant s'étend une immensité dont l'échelle prend au cœur, aux poumons, à la gorge. Nous sommes simplement trop petits pour en comprendre l'étendue. Alors tu t'adaptes et tu apprécies, tu jubiles, tu jouis, psychologiquement et physiquement. Ou tu continues à vivre sur tes anciens repères et tu subis, tu souffres, tu espères que le temps passe. J'aime ce Grand Sud, je l'adore dans toutes ses difficultés et ses beautés.

J'adore le soleil levant, mais là-bas, ça peut n'arriver qu'une fois tous les dix jours de le voir. Alors je faisais tout pour être réveillé et s'il était là, ne pas le louper.

En solitaire, tu navigues avec une dette moyenne de sommeil assez importante. Et ce qui la caractérise le plus, c'est que c'est un formidable accélérateur d'émotions. Tu passes du rire aux larmes en très peu de temps. Quand tu as des périodes où tu craques, tu vas être très bas. Mais quand tout va bien, tu planes très haut, des moments d'euphorie.

Parfois il fait beau comme nous l'entendons à terre, en Europe. Tu apprécies, ça te repose psychologiquement, tu peux à nouveau t'appuyer sur ce que tu connais… pour un temps. Car ça ne dure jamais plus de trois ou quatre heures, ça repart, le gris se réinstalle. Mais ce gris peut t'emmener loin, alors accepte-le, apprécie-le. Tu t'y perds, tu y flottes, il aiguise tes perceptions, un iota de luminosité en plus et voilà que ton humeur s'envole. On dit que la poésie se fait de tout petits riens, alors ces océans sont pure poésie… mais je suis en course.

Le temps

Michel Desjoyeaux et Samantha Davies

C'EST ÇA QUI FAIT QUE JE SUIS LÀ.

Le grand pacifique

Jean Le Cam, Armel Le Cléac'h et Vincent Riou – 2008

AU CENTRE DE SURVEILLANCE ET DE SAUVETAGE EN MER, EN FRANCE, À ÉTEL, LE SIGNAL SATELLITE EST BIEN REÇU...
... ET TRANSMIS AU CHILI, AU POSTE DE SECOURS DE PUNTA ARENAS QUI SURVEILLE LA ZONE.
VINCENT RIOU ET ARMEL LE CLÉAC'H, QUI SONT ALORS NON LOIN DU BATEAU DE JEAN LE CAM, FONT ROUTE AU PLUS VITE VERS LA POSITION.
Punta Arenas
Armel Le Cléac'h
Vincent Riou
Jean Le Cam
Pétrolier
Cap Horn
TANDIS QU'UN PÉTROLIER PASSANT PAR LÀ EST RAPIDEMENT DÉROUTÉ SUR ZONE.
NOUS SOMMES EN CONTACT VISUEL AVEC LE VOILIER. LA COQUE SEMBLE INTACTE, LE BATEAU FLOTTE, AUCUN SIGNE DE VIE.
ICI PUNTA ARENAS, POUVEZ-VOUS METTRE UN CANOT À L'EAU ET RÉCUPÉRER LE SKIPPER ? NOUS NE SAVONS PAS COMBIEN DE TEMPS IL POURRA TENIR NI QUEL EST SON ÉTAT PHYSIQUE.
METTRE UN CANOT À L'EAU DANS LES 50es... JUSTE SOUS LE CAP HORN... JE CROIS QU'ILS N'ONT PAS COMPRIS QUE NOUS NE SOMMES QUE DES MARINS DE COMMERCE, PAS DES ACROBATES.
RADIO, DONNEZ-LEUR LA SITUATION.
LE CAPITAINE VOUS INFORME QUE NOUS NE SOMMES PAS PRÉPARÉS POUR CETTE OPÉRATION. NOUS NE POUVONS RÉPONDRE QUE TRÈS DIFFICILEMENT À VOTRE DEMANDE ET EN METTANT LA VIE D'HOMMES EN DANGER.

ET PENDANT QU'ARMEL LE CLÉAC'H CRAVACHE POUR REJOINDRE JEAN LE CAM...
... VINCENT RIOU, LÉGÈREMENT EN AVANCE, ARRIVE SUR LES LIEUX.
JE SUIS SUR ZONE. MON MOTEUR EST EN CARAFE. JE TOURNE AUTOUR À LA VOILE.
À TOUS, ICI LE CENTRE DE SURVEILLANCE ET DE SECOURS DE PUNTA ARENAS. AUCUN DE NOS BATEAUX NE PEUT ARRIVER RAPIDEMENT ET NOTRE HÉLICO N'A PAS L'AUTONOMIE NÉCESSAIRE POUR VOUS REJOINDRE. AU VU DE LA SITUATION, NOUS ALLONS LANCER UNE OPÉRATION OÙ CHACUN VA AVOIR SON RÔLE À JOUER.
NOTRE HÉLICO VA DÉCOLLER DE PUNTA ARENAS AVEC DEUX PLONGEURS. DERRIÈRE LE CAP HORN, NOUS AVONS UNE RÉSERVE DE CARBURANT.
NOUS Y FERONS LE PLEIN, CE QUI NOUS PERMETTRA DE REJOINDRE LE POINT D'OPÉRATION.
ARRIVÉS SUR ZONE, NOUS DROPPERONS LES PLONGEURS.
ILS SORTIRONT LE NAVIGATEUR DU VOILIER RETOURNÉ.

ET C'EST VOUS, RIOU ET LE CLÉAC'H, QUI LES RÉCUPÉREZ. VOTRE COLLÈGUE ET NOS PLONGEURS. ENTENDU ?
ENTENDU.
L'HÉLICO SERA PROCHE DE LA PANNE SÈCHE. IL IRA SE POSER SUR LE PÉTROLIER.
QUOI ?!
POUR CE FAIRE, NOUS DEMANDONS À L'ÉQUIPAGE DE COUPER LES PARATONNERRES ET TOUS LES AUTRES ÉLÉMENTS QUI DÉPASSENT DU PONT AFIN QUE L'ON PUISSE ABORDER DANS LES MEILLEURES CONDITIONS. -- TERMINÉ. --
MAIS VOUS ME DEMANDEZ DE SACCAGER MON PROPRE BATEAU !
AH OUI, QUAND MÊME... ILS N'ONT PAS PEUR, LES GARS.
EN ATTENDANT ON VA TÂCHER DE SIGNALER NOTRE PRÉSENCE À JEAN.

BING
TIENS, LES COPAINS SONT LÀ.
BONG !
JE VAIS LEUR FAIRE COUCOU. COMME ÇA ILS VONT PEUT-ÊTRE ARRÊTER D'ABÎMER MA COQUE.
DIS DONC, C'EST ÉCRIT TOUT PETIT SUR CES FUSÉES !
LE PASSE-COQUE, A TOUT JUSTE LE BON DIAMÈTRE.
ET...
PSCHI
Ooooh !
PAF !

RÂÂÂÂH...
DE L'AIR.
JE VAIS CREVER ASPHYXIÉ, FAUT LAISSER OUVERT LE PASSE-COQUE.
IL EST DINGUE, CE MEC ! IL A FAILLI FOUTRE LE FEU À MA GRAND-VOILE !
JEAN ARRÊTE TES CONNERIES ! ON EST LÀ.
QU'EST-CE QU'Y DIT ? J'ENTENDS RIEN. ÇA A DÛ LUI FAIRE PLAISIR D'AVOIR DE MES NOUVELLES.
ARMEL, JEAN VIENT DE DONNER SIGNE DE VIE. IL PEUT SORTIR À TOUT INSTANT MAINTENANT. IL NE FAUT PLUS LE LÂCHER DES YEUX.
OK. MON MOTEUR FONCTIONNE, LAISSE-MOI LA PLACE, JE VAIS TOURNER AUTOUR DE LUI.

BON, ÇA VA PRENDRE DES HEURES À S'AÉRER ICI.
MAIS... L'EAU MONTE !
KEUF! KEUF KEUF!!
LE TROU FAIT APPEL D'AIR, LE BATEAU COULE !
ET AU MÊME INSTANT SUR LE BATEAU D'ARMEL...
BROW BROÛT!
QU'EST-CE QUI SE PASSE LÀ-DEDANS ?
?
MERDE ! LE MOTEUR SE NOIE.
ALLEZ, IL EST TEMPS D'ÉVACUER...
VINCENT, TU PEUX ME REMPLACER ? JE DOIS ALLER VOIR CE QUI SE PASSE À L'INTÉRIEUR.
SANS INFORMATION SUR L'OPÉRATION DE SECOURS MISE EN PLACE AU-DEHORS, APRÈS AVOIR MESURÉ LES RISQUES, JEAN PREND LA DÉCISION DE SORTIR.
BIEN DÉCRYPTER CHAQUE PHASE AVANT D'Y ALLER... JE N'AURAI PAS LE DROIT À L'ERREUR.

UNE GRANDE INSPIRATION...
POUSSER TOUT CE QUI ENCOMBRE LE PASSAGE.
OUVRIR LA TRAPPE DE SECOURS À L'ARRIÈRE DU BATEAU.
NAGER DANS L'EAU GELÉE, À QUELQUES ENCABLURES DU CAP HORN.

JEAN, TU NE LÂCHES TON BATEAU QUE QUAND TU ES AMARRÉ AU BOUT QUE JE T'ENVOIE.
PAS AVANT.
ET MAINTENANT...
... NE PAS RATER L'AP-PROCHE.

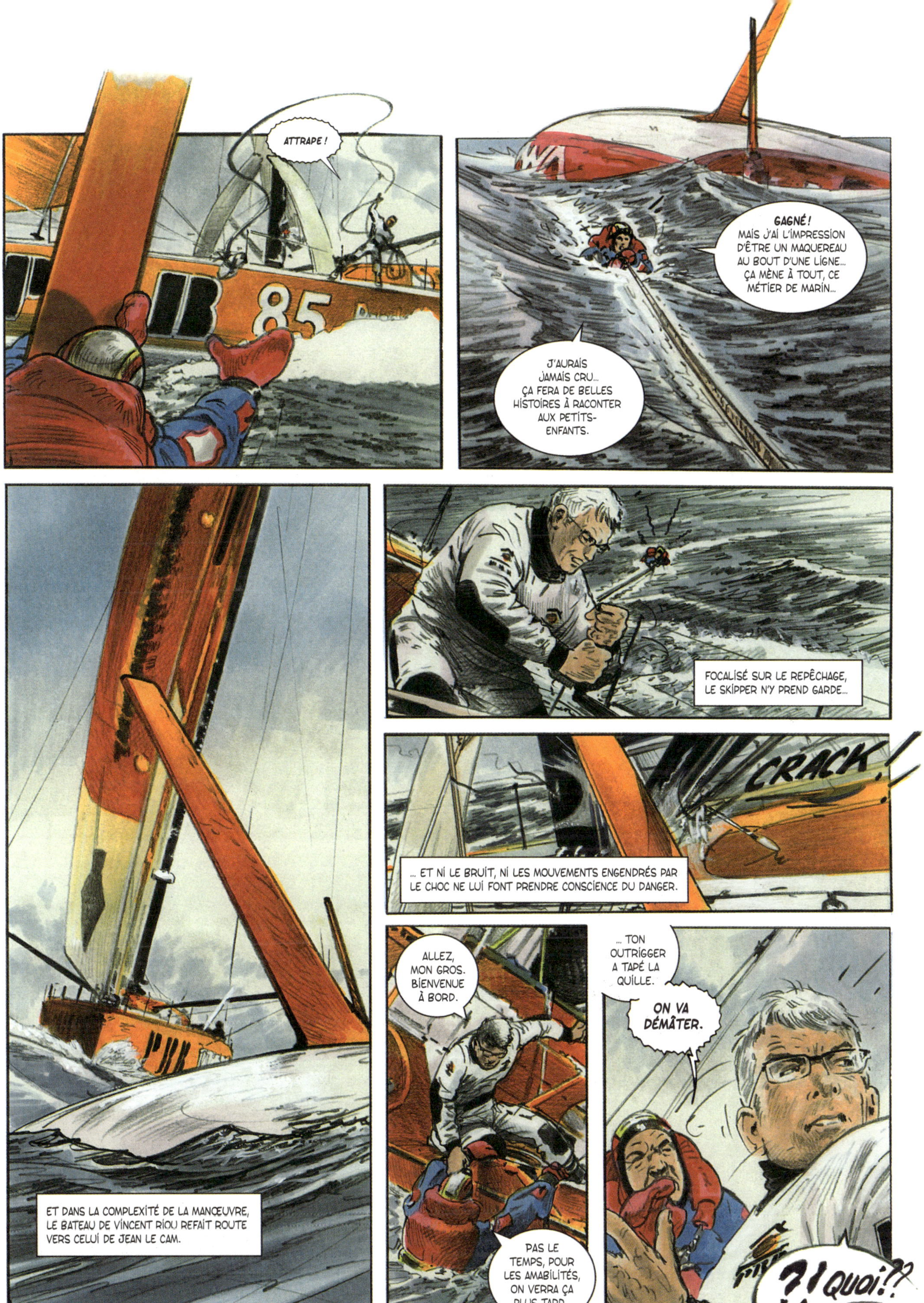
ATTRAPE !
GAGNÉ ! MAIS J'AI L'IMPRESSION D'ÊTRE UN MAQUEREAU AU BOUT D'UNE LIGNE… ÇA MÈNE À TOUT, CE MÉTIER DE MARIN…
J'AURAIS JAMAIS CRU… ÇA FERA DE BELLES HISTOIRES À RACONTER AUX PETITS-ENFANTS.
ET DANS LA COMPLEXITÉ DE LA MANŒUVRE, LE BATEAU DE VINCENT RIOU REFAIT ROUTE VERS CELUI DE JEAN LE CAM.
FOCALISÉ SUR LE REPÊCHAGE, LE SKIPPER N'Y PREND GARDE…
CRACK !
… ET NI LE BRUIT, NI LES MOUVEMENTS ENGENDRÉS PAR LE CHOC NE LUI FONT PRENDRE CONSCIENCE DU DANGER.
ALLEZ, MON GROS. BIENVENUE À BORD.
PAS LE TEMPS, POUR LES AMABILITÉS, ON VERRA ÇA PLUS TARD…
… TON OUTRIGGER A TAPÉ LA QUILLE.
ON VA DÉMÂTER.
?! QUOI !?

ET C'EST À CE MOMENT QU'ARMEL RESSORT DE SON BATEAU.
?!
LE MOTEUR FONCTIONNE, DE NOUVEAU, ON VA POUVOIR RÉCUPÉRER...
JEAN EST À BORD !
EH ! MAIS, ILS VONT DÉMÂTER !
SUR LE BATEAU DE VINCENT, SANS PERDRE UN INSTANT...
... LES DEUX MARINS RÉAGISSENT ET EMPANNENT EN CATASTROPHE.
ÇA PASSE...
LE GRÉEMENT EST À NOUVEAU EN TENSION. ÇA A L'AIR DE TENIR.
ON PEUT DIRE QUE TU SAIS MÉNAGER TES ARRIVÉES...
FAUT PAS CROIRE, C'EST BEAUCOUP D'ENTRAÎNEMENT... JE T'APPRENDRAI, TU VERRAS !
DIS DONC T'AS UNE SACRÉE TOUCHE EN COMBINAISON DE SURVIE.
T'AURAIS PAS PRIS QUELQUES KILOS ?

MAIS LES URGENCES N'ATTENDENT PAS.
ALLÔ, ANNULEZ L'OPÉRATION, ANNULEZ !
VOUS ÊTES SÛR ? ON VIENT DE DÉCOLLER DU HORN, RÉSERVOIRS PLEINS, TOUT LE MONDE EST PARÉ POUR L'INTERVENTION.
ON A RÉCUPÉRÉ JEAN. **IL EST À BORD** !!
ARMEL ? ÇA ROULE, ON EST SAUFS, JEAN EST EN PLEINE FORME.
TCHAO ET MERCI.
BRIT AIR
ARMEL LE CLÉAC'H, REPARTI EN COURSE, TERMINERA DEUXIÈME DU VENDÉE GLOBE, TANDIS QUE LE BATEAU DE VINCENT RIOU DÉMÂTERA FINALEMENT PEU APRÈS AVOIR PASSÉ LE HORN SUITE AU CHOC SUBI PAR L'OUTRIGGER. LE JURY DE COURSE LE CLASSERA TROISIÈME EN RÉPARATION DU SAUVETAGE RÉALISÉ.
DIS DONC, ELLE EST PAS MAL, TA TAMBOUILLE. JE VAIS RESTER À TON BORD PLUS LONGTEMPS QUE PRÉVU SI C'EST COMME ÇA TOUS LES JOURS.
LE CONTAINER QU'A PERCUTÉ JEAN LE CAM A DEPUIS CERTAINEMENT COULÉ, COMME NOMBRE DE SES CONGÉNÈRES QUI TOMBENT RÉGULIÈREMENT À L'EAU DEPUIS LES BATEAUX PARCOURANT LES OCÉANS.

Tu es dans une essoreuse. Depuis un mois ça secoue, ça tourne, ça te retourne, le sol droit tu as oublié ce que c'était, l'horizontal, ce foutu horizontal, tu ne t'en souviens même plus. Tu t'es cogné de partout, les bras, les épaules, les jambes, chaque articulation et la tête. La tête, tu ne comptes plus les fois où tu as été sonné, peut-être un petit évanouissement par-ci ou par-là, rapide. En fait, tu ne sais pas trop, tu ne sais plus trop, de toute façon tu es passé à autre chose, qu'importe. Cette essoreuse est froide, parfois glaciale, humide assurément, je me souviens de Desjoyeaux disant que des algues poussaient dans son cockpit!

Et puis les nuages se déchirent, dans une trouée, en hauteur, un bout de terre apparaît. Tu ne l'as plus vue depuis… depuis… pour certains depuis les Sables-d'Olonne, deux mois avant. Une falaise, pas si haute que cela d'ailleurs, mais noire, abrupte et tu as envie de la trouver fière. Les tambours et les fifres éclatent, un rayon de lumière, c'est le Horn! Le Horn! ce que l'on appelle le cap Dur, le mythe, le bout du monde et les retrouvailles avec le monde, ton monde, celui de la civilisation. C'est l'apothéose.

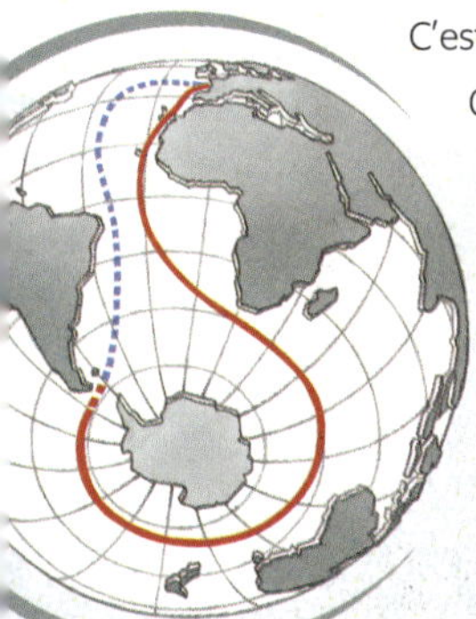

Quelque temps après, juste à la suite des klaxons venus du ciel, quelqu'un, tu ne sais qui, appuie sur le bouton stop de cette foutue essoreuse. Et après le grand chut des instruments à vent, le tambour s'arrête à son tour, se stabilise, le bateau se redresse. Ça s'arrête, enfin!, en tout cas, c'est l'impression que tu as. Tout s'arrête et tu as beau être en course, tu t'en moques royalement, tout s'arrête et tu es bien. Le calme, le grand calme, coooool, tu te rappelles que les humains sont faits pour vivre sur leurs deux jambes et pas à quatre pattes. À tes oreilles, soudain le silence est la plus belle des musiques. C'est d'un repos! Et ça dure comme cela jusqu'au détroit de Le Maire, trois heures d'une navigation tranquille, lente.

Et puis ça repart… évidemment, forcément. Tu es en course et il ne s'agirait pas de te faire rattraper.

C'est beau, non? Je l'ai doublé plusieurs fois le Horn et je peux te dire que ça ne s'est jamais passé comme ça. Mais je ne peux pas faire autrement, c'est comme ça que je veux te le raconter. C'est un mythe. Pour tout le monde, pour tous les navigateurs et les navigatrices, c'est le Horn! l'unique, le seul. La puissance d'un mythe, c'est qu'il est au-dessus de la réalité. Je le repasserai peut-être encore plusieurs fois dans ma vie ce fameux cap et je crois que toujours, le passage ultime aura la saveur du passage que je viens de te décrire. Le Horn, c'est le caillou, la falaise, l'avancée vers le Sud, la terre promise quand tu viens de traverser les océans avec lui seul pour ligne de mire, le mythe de l'aboutissement, la sortie de l'enfer. Même quand tes mers du Sud n'ont pas été l'enfer, tu le ressens comme la sortie du maelström. Parce que si ça ne l'a pas été, ça aurait pu l'être, l'enfer. Le Horn est porté par son conditionnel. Parfois tu le passes et tu ne le vois même pas, c'est la nuit ou tu en es trop loin, mais ça reste le Horn. La légende.

C'est comme quand tu es sur l'autoroute et que tu sors. Tout d'un coup tu passes de 130 km/h à 90 et "Oh, on se traîne." Tu n'as plus les mêmes références, il faut se réadapter. C'est un peu dur mentalement.

C'est dur aussi le Horn. Tout le monde te fait la fête, te dit que ça y est, tu es sorti, l'arrivée se profile. Toi aussi d'ailleurs tu n'échappes pas à cette sorte d'euphorie même si tu sais que c'est faux. Bien entendu c'est faux, ta raison essaye de te le rappeler, tu le sais mais tu n'arrives pas à l'accepter, le sentiment du mythe du Horn

Pour moi, on n'est pas des cap-horniers parce qu'on le fait dans le "bon sens", on le passe dans le sens des vents. Et nos bateaux n'ont rien à voir avec ceux de la grande époque qui ont fait le mythe. Avant, ils perdaient 25 hommes au passage !... Mais oui, le Cap Horn, c'est le Cap Horn, la fin des mers du Sud, l'Everest. Notre Everest.

couplé à l'aboutissement des mers du Sud est plus fort que ta raison. Au fur et à mesure de la course, tu t'es mis des buts à atteindre pour te motiver et là, le Horn, c'est le dernier point que tu avais à atteindre avant les Sables-d'Olonne. Donc ça y est, banco, tu y es. Sauf que pas du tout, tu as encore l'Atlantique Sud et Nord à parcourir, un mois de mer, tu n'en es qu'au tiers de ta course. Alors le cap Horn, ça rime aussi avec une baisse de motivation, et pas sûr qu'un seul skipper ait pu ne pas tomber un instant dans cette lassitude.

Tu étais à dix-huit, vingt nœuds et plus, depuis trente jours, un mois entier, c'est long un mois non-stop, et d'un coup, tu ralentis. Tu n'as jamais été aussi près de l'arrivée et tu as l'impression de n'avoir jamais été aussi lent et aussi loin. Tu t'es habitué aux grandes vitesses et le retour à une réalité, disons plus connue et donc normale pour nous marins de l'Atlantique Nord, est dur à accepter.

Mais le Cap Horn, malgré tes sentiments qui peuvent être divergents, ça reste un des moments les plus forts de ta course. Son passage valide les choix que tu as faits, avec ton équipe, sur l'inconnu, sur l'invalidable. Personne ne va s'entraîner dans le Grand Sud pour préparer son bateau. Il n'y a que les supputations, l'expérience, le flair, qui t'ont amené là, jusqu'à la porte de sortie de cet univers. Victoire sur tous les paris inconnus.

Tu n'avances pas et tu es content. Et ça ! C'est énorme. Tu souffles, tout le corps se relâche. Ça fait un mois que tu ne fais qu'attaquer et là, pfuuu... C'est digne d'une séance de sophrologie.

Et il y a aussi le passage du Horn en pleine tempête... alors, sors-toi du danger et après seulement tu pourras ressentir le mythe, souffler, savoir qu'il est désormais dans ton sillage. Tu ne l'auras pas vu mais, dans des conditions dantesques, alors peut-être l'auras-tu encore plus ressenti.

C’est le dernier objectif avant la ligne d’arrivée. C’est important. Le mythe et la légende. Il y a ceux qui l’ont salué, et ceux qui ne l’ont pas salué.

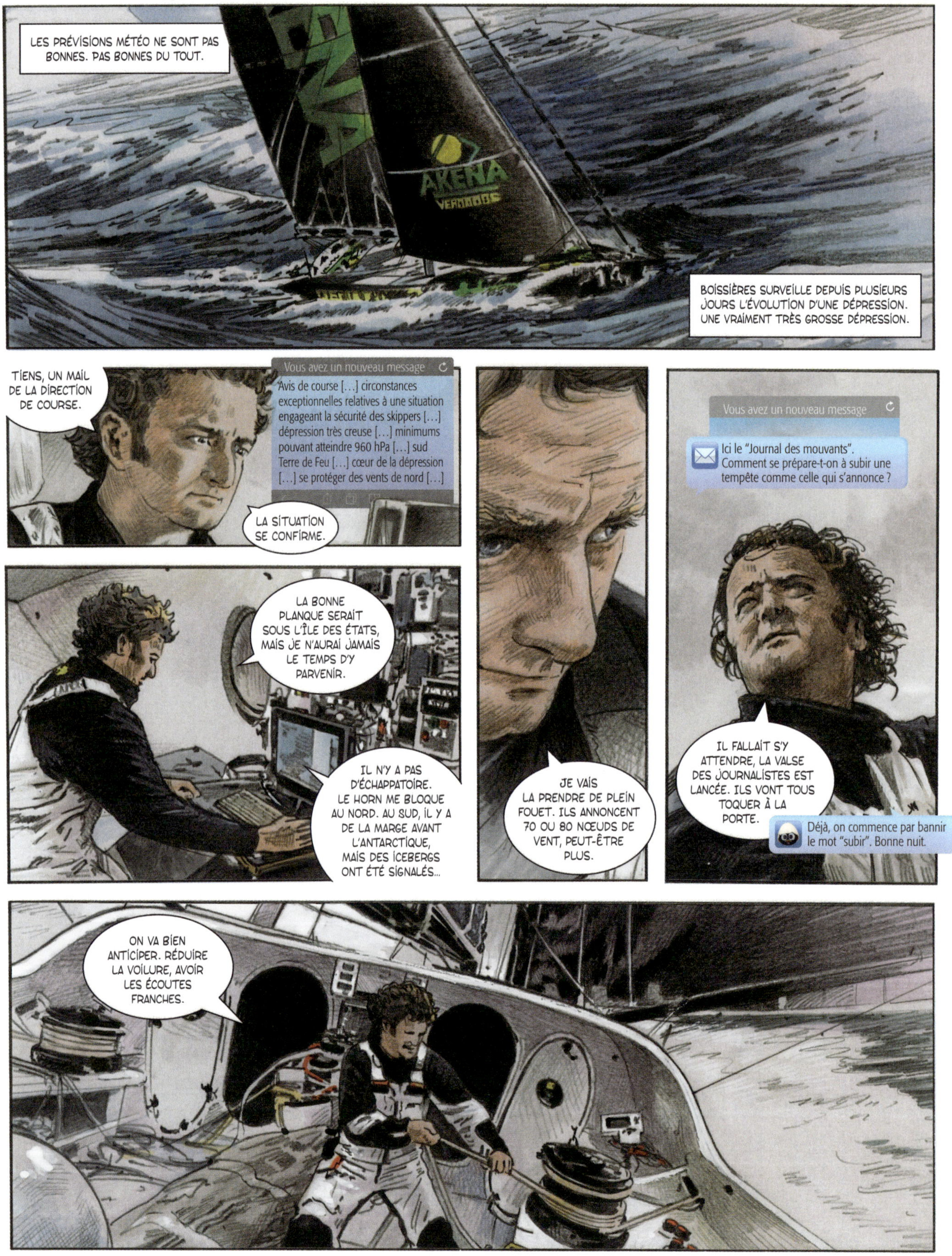
LES PRÉVISIONS MÉTÉO NE SONT PAS BONNES. PAS BONNES DU TOUT.
AKENA
BOISSIÈRES SURVEILLE DEPUIS PLUSIEURS JOURS L'ÉVOLUTION D'UNE DÉPRESSION. UNE VRAIMENT TRÈS GROSSE DÉPRESSION.
TIENS, UN MAIL DE LA DIRECTION DE COURSE.
Vous avez un nouveau message
Avis de course [...] circonstances exceptionnelles relatives à une situation engageant la sécurité des skippers [...] dépression très creuse [...] minimums pouvant atteindre 960 hPa [...] sud Terre de Feu [...] cœur de la dépression [...] se protéger des vents de nord [...]
LA SITUATION SE CONFIRME.
Vous avez un nouveau message
Ici le "Journal des mouvants". Comment se prépare-t-on à subir une tempête comme celle qui s'annonce ?
LA BONNE PLANQUE SERAIT SOUS L'ÎLE DES ÉTATS, MAIS JE N'AURAI JAMAIS LE TEMPS D'Y PARVENIR.
IL N'Y A PAS D'ÉCHAPPATOIRE. LE HORN ME BLOQUE AU NORD. AU SUD, IL Y A DE LA MARGE AVANT L'ANTARCTIQUE, MAIS DES ICEBERGS ONT ÉTÉ SIGNALÉS...
JE VAIS LA PRENDRE DE PLEIN FOUET. ILS ANNONCENT 70 OU 80 NŒUDS DE VENT, PEUT-ÊTRE PLUS.
IL FALLAIT S'Y ATTENDRE, LA VALSE DES JOURNALISTES EST LANCÉE. ILS VONT TOUS TOQUER À LA PORTE.
Déjà, on commence par bannir le mot "subir". Bonne nuit.
ON VA BIEN ANTICIPER. RÉDUIRE LA VOILURE, AVOIR LES ÉCOUTES FRANCHES.

RANGER LE PONT AU MAXIMUM, NE RIEN LAISSER DEHORS.
ÊTRE PRÊT À ÊTRE À SEC DE TOILE, ENROULEUR CLAIR.
TOUT ARRIMER DANS LA SOUTE À VOILES, QUE RIEN N'AMPLIFIE LE ROULIS ET LE TANGAGE.
Ici le "Journal du samedi". Question simple : un skipper du Vendée Globe, ça a peur parfois ?
Bonjour. J'aimerais savoir ce que vous avez prévu dans le cas où le bateau se retourne.
votre bateau dé… sans quille
est-il tou…
D'APRÈS LES FICHIERS, LA DÉPRESSION NE DÉSENFLE PAS, LA TRAJECTOIRE SE CONFIRME…
Je suis aux abonnés absents. Tchao, bonsoir, à la r'voyure.
SI J'ESSAYE DE LA LONGER ELLE SERA MOINS FORTE, MAIS ÇA VA DURER DES PLOMBES. SINON IL Y A LA POSSIBILITÉ DE LA COUPER…
J'ENTRE DANS LE FRONT. GROSSE BASTON, MAIS COURTE. J'ARRIVE AU CENTRE DE LA DÉPRESSION, C'EST LÀ OÙ CE SERA LE PLUS CALME. ENSUITE, IL FAUT QUE J'EN RESSORTE, DEUXIÈME COUP DE BASTON…
MOUAIS… UNE RACLÉE, JE SOUFFLE, UNE RACLÉE.
SE JETER DANS LA GUEULE DU LOUP…
?!
TULU TULULU…
ÇA Y EST ! JE NE RÉPONDS PLUS AUX MAILS, ALORS ILS PASSENT PAR LE TÉLÉPHONE.

ICI RADIO "CÂLINE", VOUS ALLEZ BIEN ?
ÇA VA DÉPENDRE DE VOTRE QUESTION.
J'AIMERAIS CONNAÎTRE VOTRE TEMPS ESTIMÉ DE SURVIE SI VOUS TOMBEZ À L'EAU ?
QUOI ?!!
ALLEZ, ON ARRÊTE LES BÊTISES. FIN DES COMMUNICATIONS. ILS VONT COMMENCER À ME FAIRE TROP GAMBERGER, CEUX-LÀ.
CLIC !
COMBINAISON DE SURVIE.
FERMER TOUT.
KLONG !
BIEN CLOISONNER.
ET ATTENDRE LA PREMIÈRE CARTOUCHE...
ÇA Y EST, LA DÉPRESSION EST SUR NOUS, ON Y EST.

ÇA A L'AIR DE SE CALMER UN PEU. ON EST AU CŒUR DE L'OURAGAN. CALME RELATIF.
JETER UN ŒIL POUR CONTRÔLER L'ÉTAT DU BATEAU.
RIEN À SIGNALER. TOUT SEMBLE TENIR. PARÉ POUR LA DEUXIÈME CLAQUE.

ATTENDRE À NOUVEAU.
ÇA S'AGITE DEHORS! EN AVANT POUR LE DEUXIÈME TOUR D'ESSOREUSE.
BLAM!
KLONG!!
HOW!

ET AU BOUT D'HEURES INTERMINABLES.
LA MER, L'AIR, LE BATEAU LAVÉS PAR LES FURIES...
OUF ! ÇA FAIT DU BIEN DE SORTIR.
ET RIEN NE SEMBLE CASSÉ.
C'EST BEAU MALGRÉ TOUT.
METTRE TOUS CES MESSAGES À LA POUBELLE. ILS M'ONT BIEN FAIT MONTER LA PRESSION, CES ANDOUILLES. À FORCE, J'ÉTAIS À DEUX DOIGTS DE SURRÉAGIR ET ALORS... L'ACCIDENT N'EST JAMAIS LOIN.
JE SUIS CREVÉ ! GROS COUP DE BARRE. JE M'ACCORDE UNE BONNE HEURE DE SOMMEIL ET C'EST REPARTI !
LE JOUR EST REVENU, LA TEMPÊTE S'EN EST ALLÉE ET LA COURSE ÉTAIT TOUJOURS EN COURS.
« ON SAIT NAVIGUER AVEC NOS BATEAUX. L'ENJEU, C'EST D'ANTICIPER TOUT EN RESTANT SEREIN, REFUSER LA MAUVAISE PRESSION, CELLE QUI VIENT DE L'EXTÉRIEUR. »

Pour quelques heures… Armel Le Cléac'h et François Gabart – 2012

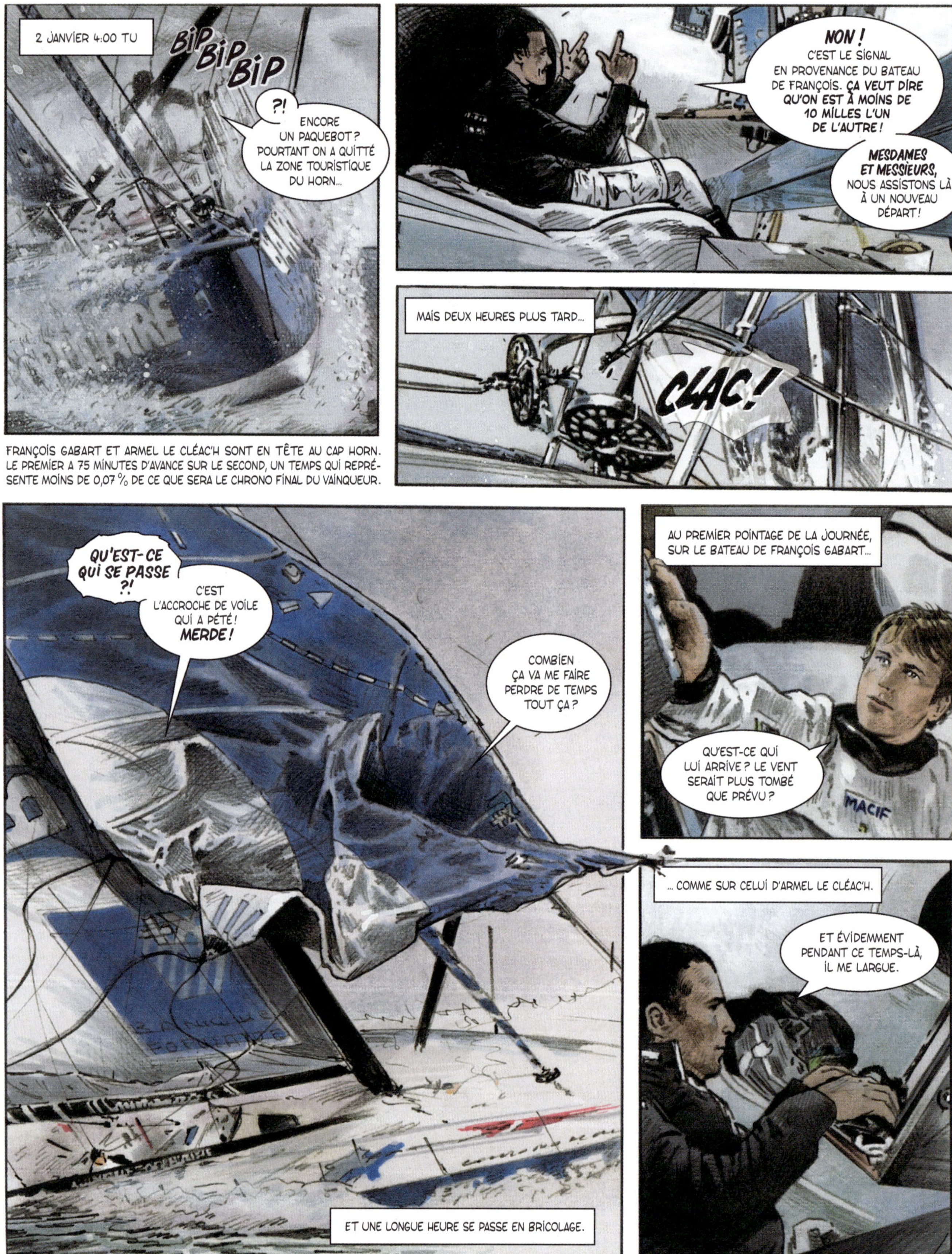

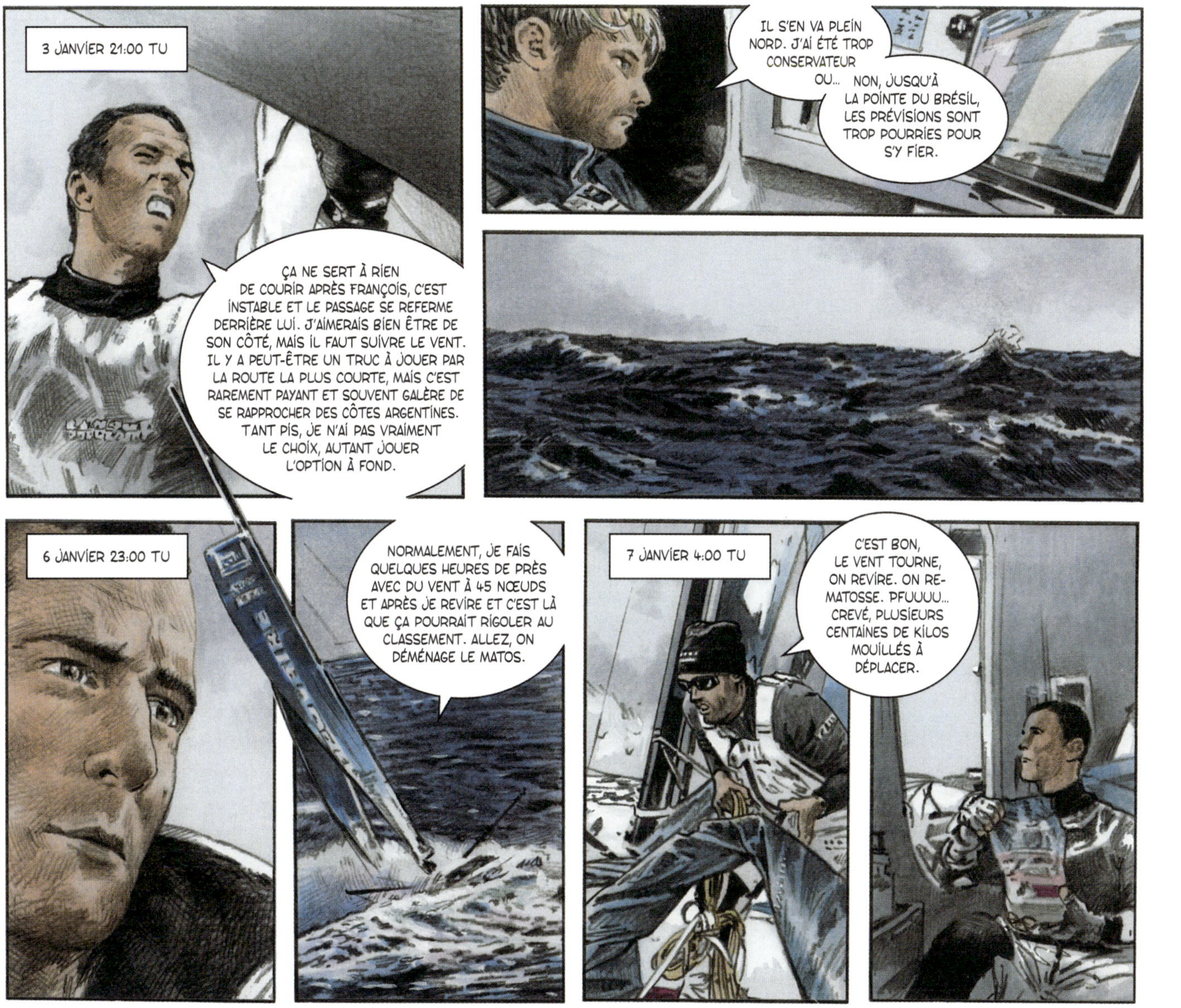

JAMAIS ARMEL, EMBARQUÉ DE FAIT DANS UNE VEINE DE VENT INSTABLE, NE RÉUSSIRA À RATTRAPER SON ADVERSAIRE. LE 3 JANVIER, IL COMPTAIT 40 MILLES D'ÉCART AVEC FRANÇOIS. LE 9 JANVIER, ALORS QU'ILS SONT À NOUVEAU ALIGNÉS SUR LA MÊME TRAJECTOIRE, C'EST 140 MILLES QUE L'ON CONSTATE ENTRE LES DEUX. ARMEL LE CLÉAC'H FINIRA DEUXIÈME AUX SABLES-D'OLONNE, 3 HEURES 17 MINUTES ET 12 SECONDES DERRIÈRE FRANÇOIS GABART, UN ÉCART DE 43 MILLES LES SÉPARAIT ALORS. CELA FAISAIT 78 JOURS, 2 HEURES ET 16 MINUTES QU'ILS SE DISPUTAIENT LA PREMIÈRE PLACE.

Te voilà à nouveau dans l'Atlantique, celui que tu penses connaître. Tes moyennes chutent d'un coup, c'est dur pour le moral car après le Horn, rien n'est facile On est tout de même à dix, douze, quinze nœuds avec une mer plus petite, plus courte, plus hachée. Les changements météo sont plus fréquents, il y a des bascules, tu affines cent fois tes trajectoires. Après le Horn, cest dur. L'Atlantique t'est familier, mais tu avais oublié à quel point il est technique et sollicitant.

Tu te retrouves au large de l'Argentine, là où naissent nombre des dépressions qui t'ont porté dans les mers du Sud. Elles ne sont pas encore violentes, tu ne risques pas le trop gros coup de baston, par contre le chaos le plus complet, oui. Les prévisions météo sont souvent approximatives avec des phénomènes locaux courts mais violents. Des orages aux éclairs fournis, tu ne fais pas le malin dans ton rafiot avec le mât et son gréement proprement pointés vers le ciel, véritable appel métallique à la foudre. Dominique Wavre, Javier Sansó et Arnaud Boissières, en 2012, coupent toute leur électronique de bord, et avancent à l'aveugle en espérant que le trait électrique venu du ciel tombera à côté.

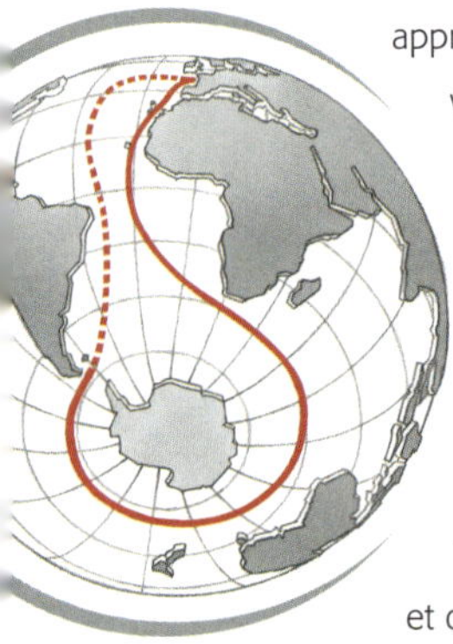

Tu enchaînes par la remontée du Brésil. À force, on connaît et on espère que la route qui passe bien à l'écart des côtes sera ouverte. Ce n'est pas la plus courte, mais les prévisions y sont sûres, le vent régulier et la mer rangée. C'est propre, tu vas relativement vite, tu ne sollicites pas trop le bateau. Et surtout, il faut la comparer à son alter ego, celle qui longe les côtes brésiliennes. Là, tu le sais, le calvaire est annoncé, tu vas porter ta croix pour les jours à venir. Des vents qui basculent sans arrêt, un coup au près, un coup au portant, un coup sans vent, avec une mer casse-bateau qui te fait mal, complètement hachée, ça craque, ça grince, ça tape, ça tape, ça tape. Tu slalomes entre les plates-formes pétrolières, c'est moche ces grandes araignées de métal fixées raides à la mer. Le bordel, en plus de tout ça, ce sont les pêcheurs et leurs filets... La nuit tu as des lumières qui clignotent de partout et de toutes les couleurs, avec le bateau qui fait la gigue tu ne comprends plus rien. "Je passe au cul de celui-là ou par-devant?", "Et son feu jaune, il est vert ou rouge? Bâbord ou tribord?"... la VHF gueule en portugais, je ne comprends pas un mot, juste que c'est contre moi qu'ils en ont, mais qu'est-ce que tu veux, je ne fais pas ce que je veux dans ces conditions, juste ce que je peux.

Enfin, c'est la course et tu as beau vivre l'enfer, tu l'as voulue et tu sais qu'à la fin, si tu n'as pas fait n'importe quoi en choisissant ta route, tu devrais en sortir gagnant. Pour s'engouffrer là-dedans, il faut être absolument sûr du gain de l'option météo.

Tu n'arrives pas à avancer. Tu n'as pas de solution. Tu essayes toutes les possibilités imaginables, tu ballastes devant, tu ballastes derrière et la situation change... Tant qu'à faire, t'essayes de te reposer, tu te fais un café, mais le café, il ne reste pas dans la tasse. Alors il n'y a qu'à attendre. Tu attends.

Dans la remontée de l'Atlantique, il y a un autre gros morceau qui va te tomber dessus, c'est l'état de ton bateau. Dans le Sud, tu as réparé au jour le jour ce qui cassait, mais souvent les conditions de mer, et, surtout, le froid, t'ont dirigé vers le bout de ficelle plutôt que la règle de l'art. Finalement pendant toute cette chevauchée autour de l'Antarctique, tu as poussé ton bateau plus qu'ailleurs mais d'une manière relativement stable, peu de changements de voiles, peu de passages d'un extrême

à l'autre. Ici, retour à la polyvalence, tu vas retrouver tout le panel des conditions qui vont solliciter ton bateau. Tendre, détendre, changer, visser, dévisser, régler et re-régler. Si ton bateau s'est dégradé au fil du temps sans réelles conséquences jusqu'ici, là c'est le moment de l'addition. Le "petit-problème" que tu avais va lâcher, faire cascade et se transformer en gros, gros handicap. Ajoute à cela que ton organisme commence à être crevé et tu as le cocktail parfait pour perdre la niaque, baisser les bras, la saute d'humeur et peut-être même l'abandon ne sont pas loin. Ressaisis-toi camarade !

Le matériel se souvient. En fin de course, il y a beaucoup de petites avaries qui sont de l'ordre de l'usure et de la fatigue.

Non, à terre en suivant la course, peut-être que l'on se dit que la partie est jouée, que le plus dur est fait, mais en mer, les Atlantiques au retour, c'est long, usant, un calvaire.

Une fois sorti du Brésil, tu passes l'équateur, le Pot-au-Noir n'est pas actif en cette saison. Puis tu as l'anticyclone des Açores sur ta route, les fichiers météo prévoient à long terme, tu vas le contourner en montant très haut au nord, jusqu'à la latitude de l'Irlande – parfois oui, de l'Irlande ! – où tu vas pouvoir l'enrouler au plus près de la route directe et alors, tu souris.

Facile, non ? Non. Définitivement, la remontée des Atlantiques est une tannée. La tannée qui fait la beauté du Vendée Globe, qui donne toute sa puissance au dicton que tant que la ligne d'arrivée n'est pas franchie, tout peut arriver. Le golfe de Gascogne est sur ton chemin, le fameux, tu le retrouves, celui que tu connais tant, ton meilleur ennemi. Et là, ça peut être très costaud. C'est le même golfe que lors du départ, la même probabilité et capacité de tempête, sauf que tu es crevé, sauf que ton bateau est crevé, sauf que demain, ou dans quelques jours au plus, tu arrives. En 2008, là où Armel Le Cléac'h casse le plus de matériel, c'est en se prenant une prune au retour dans le Gascogne… et combien arrivent sans quille, sans grand-voile… sans…

Le Vendée Globe est une course par élimination et l'histoire montre qu'elle commence le jour du départ et qu'elle finit le jour de l'arrivée.

Mais à la fin, tu as cette ligne à franchir. Et là… et là… la remontée de l'Atlantique, c'est magique.

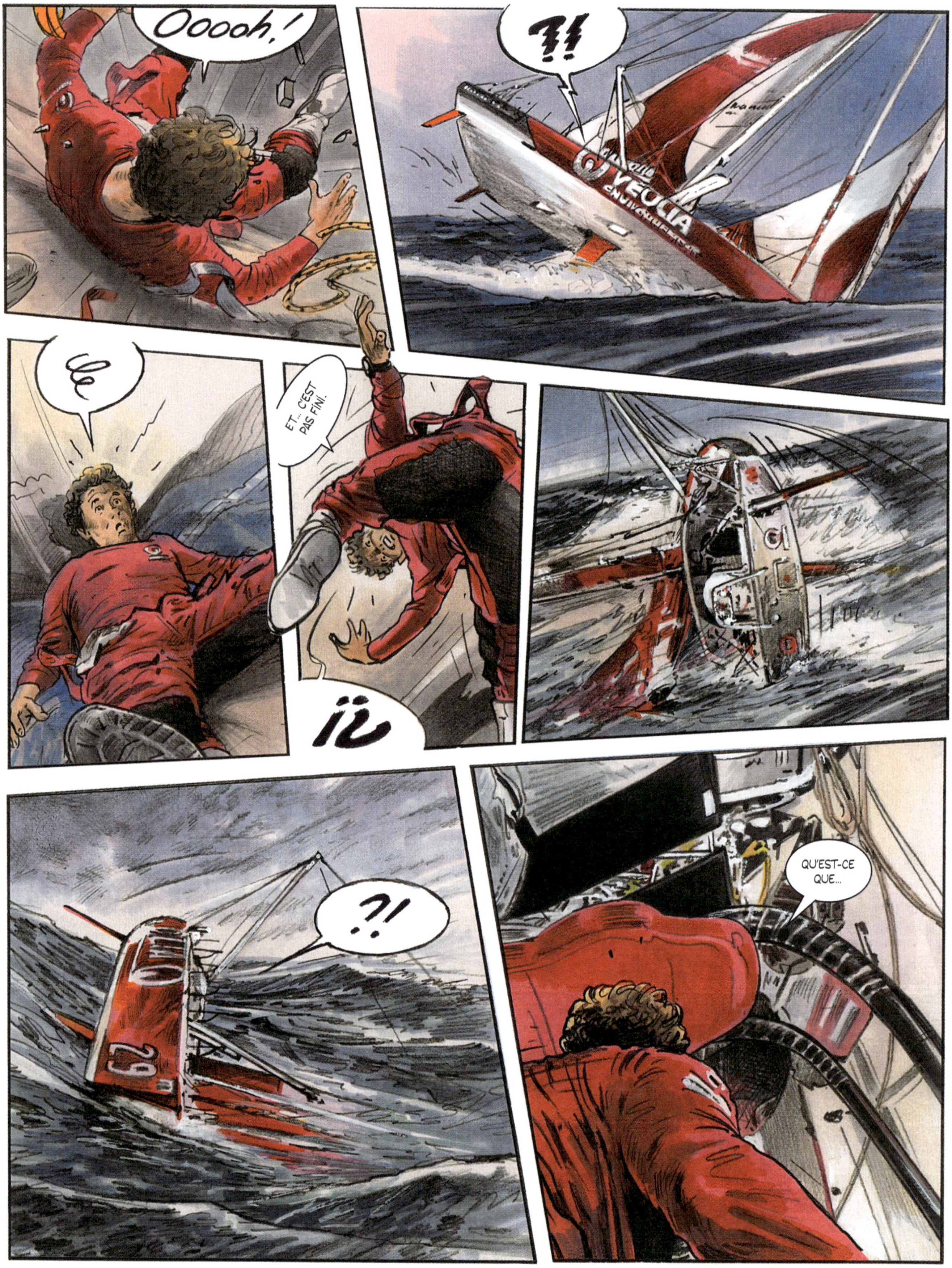
Ooooh !
?!!
ET... C'EST PAS FINI.
?!
QU'EST-CE QUE...

JE SORS, LA MER EST ROUGE. ROUGE, TOUT AUTOUR DU BATEAU.
UN REGARD À L'ARRIÈRE ET...

... L'ÉNORME MASSE.
C'EST PAS POSSIBLE !
!

LE TEMPS DE REMETTRE LE BATEAU À PLAT...
J'AI TAPÉ UNE BALEINE! MERDE, DANS QUEL ÉTAT EST-ELLE ?
MAIS!? ET LE BATEAU ?
VITE !
LES SAFRANS ?
LES DÉRIVES ?
LA QUILLE ?
LES ÉTAIS ?
NON, TOUT VA BIEN À L'EXTÉRIEUR. VOYONS L'INTÉRIEUR.
LES CLOISONS ?
AH ! MINCE... C'EST PAS JOLI, ÇA...
NICO, HUBERT, VA FALLOIR M'AIDER. UN CÉTACÉ EST TOMBÉ AMOUREUX DE MA QUILLE...
... ILS ONT DÛ VOULOIR SE FAIRE UN DÎNER AUX CHANDELLES. ILS SE SONT SERVIS DU VOILE DE QUILLE COMME OUVRE-BOÎTE. LA CLOISON CENTRALE A BOUGÉ.
T'ES MAL... C'EST LÀ OÙ EST REPRISE LA COMPRESSION DU GRÉEMENT. ÇA REPRÉSENTE PLUSIEURS TONNES DE PRESSION...
SI ÇA LÂCHE... LE MÂT TRAVERSE LA COQUE ET EMBARQUE LA QUILLE AVEC LUI POUR LE GRAND PLONGEON.
AH...

L'AFFAIRE SEMBLAIT BÂCHÉE POUR TOUT LE MONDE. MAIS IL FALLAIT TOUT DE MÊME QUE JE RENTRE. ET À PART NAVIGUER, IL N'Y A QU'UNE CHOSE QUE JE SACHE À PEU PRÈS FAIRE, C'EST CONSTRUIRE DES BATEAUX. ALORS TANT QU'À FAIRE, AUTANT M'OCCUPER.
TAK TAK TAK
SCRITCH SCRATCH !
J'AI MIS LE CASQUE DE MINEUR ET JE SUIS ALLÉ AU TURBIN. NOUS, ON N'A PAS DE CHARBON MAIS ON A DU CARBONE. QUAND TU LE TRAVAILLES, TU LE PONCES ET TU AS DE LA POUSSIÈRE NOIRE QUI SE RÉPAND PARTOUT, QUI SE COLLE, QUI S'ACCROCHE. TU STRATIFIES, TU AS DE LA PÂTE VISQUEUSE ET AU NIVEAU DE LA CLOISON, TU N'AS PAS UN BRIN DE LUMIÈRE, TOUT À LA FRONTALE.
J'AI COMMENCÉ PAR FAIRE LE COMPTE DE TOUT LE CARBONE QUE J'AVAIS À MA DISPOSITION. LE MATÉRIEL DE RECHANGE ET LE MATÉRIEL QUI N'ÉTAIT PAS STRICTEMENT INDISPENSABLE. MODIFIER ET CRÉER UNE FORME, ÇA N'EST PAS TRÈS DUR, MAIS REPRENDRE LES POINTS DE COMPRESSION... POUR MOI, C'ÉTAIT UN GROS CHALLENGE. TOUTE LA STRUCTURE AVAIT BOUGÉ.
JE ME SUIS ENSUITE ATTAQUÉ AU PUITS DE QUILLE. BOUCHER LES FISSURES PUIS LE CONSOLIDER. ET ENFIN, J'AI REFAIT L'ÉTANCHÉITÉ. L'EAU ENTRAIT DEPUIS LE CHOC ET TOUTE LA PARTIE BASSE DU CHANTIER ÉTAIT IMMERGÉE. HEUREUSEMENT QU'IL ME RESTAIT DE LA RÉSINE QUI SE TRAVAILLE MÊME DANS L'EAU.
J'AI REFAIT TOUTE LA CLOISON ET LE CORNIÉRAGE SUR LA PARTIE SUPÉRIEURE. J'AI MIS LES LATTES RECOUPÉES EN ÉVENTAIL, DU HAUT VERS LE BAS. L'AJUSTEMENT DEVAIT VRAIMENT ÊTRE AU MILLIMÈTRE POUR QUE LA PRESSION SE DIFFUSE BIEN TOUT DU LONG. PUIS J'AI DÛ RESOLIDARISER L'ENSEMBLE AVEC LA COQUE. TOUT ÉTAIT PÉTÉ, PLUS RIEN N'ÉTAIT JOINTIF.
OUF ! ÇA A L'AIR DE TENIR.
ET PENDANT CE TEMPS-LÀ, LE SYSTÈME MÉTÉO ÉTAIT EN TRAIN DE CHANGER. IL COMMENÇAIT À FAIRE CHAUD, C'EST MIEUX QUE LE FROID, ASSURÉMENT ! MAIS... J'ÉTAIS NOIR DE CARBONE, VISQUEUX DE SUEUR, HUMIDE D'EAU STAGNANTE...
ÇA A ÉTÉ TROIS JOURS D'EFFORTS SANS RELÂCHE ET À LA FIN JE N'AVAIS PLUS UN GRAMME DE RÉSINE OU DE TISSU DISPONIBLE À BORD. FRANCHEMENT, J'AI BIEN MORFLÉ.
ALLEZ, TOUT DOUX, ÇA REPART.
ÇA Y EST, LE VENT D'OUEST REVIENT, ANTICYCLONE PASSÉ.
DIS DONC, IL EST LONG CE POT-AU-NOIR, DEUX JOURS ENGLUÉS.
JE REBORDE.
PARFAIT.
JE REBORDE.

J'ÉTAIS À NOUVEAU EN COURSE ! C'ÉTAIT INESPÉRÉ. MAIS TROIS SEMAINES APRÈS LA RÉPARATION...
CROUIIIIII
?!
OOOOH !
'TAIN ÇA GÎTE DRÔLEMENT.
J'VOIS RIEN.
Y A PLUS DE QUILLE ! ON VA CHAVIRER...
ET SI JE GÎTE UN PEU PLUS ?
JOUER AVEC LES 3 TONNES DE LA COQUE...
... REMPLIR LES BALLASTS, 5 TONNES D'EAU À FOND DE CALE.
... LA DEMI-TONNE DE GRÉEMENT...
TAP! TAP!
... LA CLOISON AVAIT TENU BON, LE MÂT ÉTAIT RESTÉ EN PLACE, MAIS LE CHOC AU NIVEAU DE LA QUILLE, LENTEMENT, AVAIT FISSURÉ L'ATTACHE DU BULBE QUI A CÉDÉ.
ÇA DEVRAIT COMPENSER LE LEVIER DU VENT DANS LES VOILES...
OOOOH ! ÇA DÉRAPE, ÇA CHASSE, C'EST DEVENU UNE VRAIE PATINOIRE !

IL VA FALLOIR TENIR LE BATEAU SI JE VEUX QU'IL RESTE À L'ENDROIT.
DU DOIGTÉ, DE LA PRÉCISION, BIEN ANTICIPER LES SAUTES DE VENT… LE MATCH N'EST PAS FINI !
EN FAIT, C'EST PLUTÔT AGRÉABLE DE NAVIGUER SANS QUILLE…
… ÇA GLISSE TOUT EN LÉGÈRETÉ.
5000 MILLES PARCOURUS DEPUIS LA RENCONTRE AVEC LE CÉTACÉ. JE NE VOULAIS PAS LÂCHER MAINTENANT, PAS APRÈS AVOIR RÉUSSI UN PAREIL CHANTIER.
RETOUR À L'ÉCOLE DE VOILE !
DE JOLIS SOUVENIRS
C'EST COMME NAVIGUER EN OPTIMIST, ON SE CROIRAIT À LA PLAGE…
MAIS AVEC UN BATEAU UN PEU PLUS GRAND…
… OU UN SKIPPER PLUS PETIT.
QUESTION DE POINT DE VUE.
J'AI TENU ENCORE 600 MILLES, MAIS ARRIVÉ AUX AÇORES, LES PRÉVISIONS MÉTÉO SE SONT DÉGRADÉES AVEC UNE MER TRÈS CREUSE À VENIR. C'ÉTAIT UN GROS RISQUE À COURIR POUR LE BATEAU ET, POTENTIELLEMENT, LA MISE EN DANGER DES SECOURS SI JE VENAIS À LES APPELER. J'ÉTAIS DEUXIÈME AU CLASSEMENT, MICH' ÉTAIT SUR LE POINT D'ARRIVER AUX SABLES-D'OLONNE, VICTORIEUX, ET J'ÉTAIS ÉPUISÉ… J'AI DIT STOP, J'AI JETÉ L'ÉPONGE À QUELQUES MILLES DE L'ARRIVÉE.

ET UN BEAU JOUR, ON NE SAÎT PLUS POURQUOÎ, ON NE SAÎT PLUS COMMENT, C'EST L'ARRÎVÉE.

101

« IL N'Y A PAS DEUX VENDÉE GLOBE PAREIL. À CHAQUE FOIS
C'EST UNE AVENTURE DIFFÉRENTE. »

« LE VENDÉE GLOBE, TU Y MONTRES CE QUE TU VEUX, MAIS SURTOUT TU Y MONTRES CE QUE TU PEUX. »
« SUR CETTE COURSE, LE GÉNÉRAL N'EXISTE PAS. IL Y A 10, 20 OU 30 COUREURS, MAIS SI TU CHERCHES À EN TIRER UNE MOYENNE ALORS TU ES PERDU. TU NE POURRAS JAMAIS COMPRENDRE CE QU'EST CETTE COURSE...

... CE N'EST PAS UN MONOLITHE, ET C'EST ÇA QUI FAIT LA VALEUR DU VENDÉE GLOBE. »

« PAR SA DURÉE, C'EST UNE DES DERNIÈRES COURSES OÙ TU DOIS RÉELLEMENT COMPOSER AVEC LES ÉLÉMENTS. NE PAS FORCER. TU PARS ET TU N'AS AUCUNE IDÉE DE CE QUI SE PASSERA DANS DEUX, TROIS SEMAINES, UN MOIS… POUR VIVRE CETTE COURSE, IL FAUT SE MOUVOIR DANS LES ÉLÉMENTS, CHERCHER UNE OSMOSE. »
« ON PASSE SANS ARRÊT DU PIRE MOMENT AU MEILLEUR. C'EST UNE COURSE DE CONTRASTE, ET C'EST ÇA QUI EST LE PLUS BEAU. »

ET PARFOIS...
IL Y A DES MOMENTS MAGNIFIQUES.

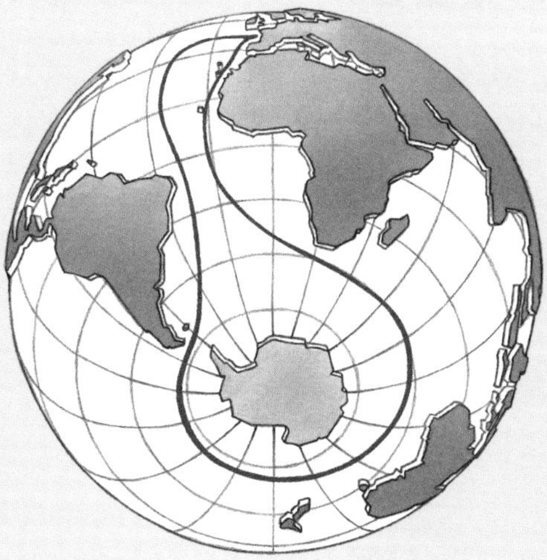

6 NOVEMBRE 2016

VENDÉE GLOBE – 8e ÉDITION

Le 6 novembre 2016, trente bateaux s'élancent pour le tour du monde.

Sur ces trente, la moitié des prétendants sont des récidivistes, parmi lesquels on en dénombre cinq qui s'y attaquent pour la quatrième fois ! L'éventail des âges n'aura jamais été aussi large, allant de 23 à 66 ans avec d'excellents régatiers et des bateaux intelligemment préparés. Malheureusement, le fait le plus marquant de cette édition est qu'aucune skippeuse ne sera au départ. Ce n'est pourtant pas faute de candidates sérieuses, d'excellent niveau sportif et de grande expérience…

Voici un panel d'informations qui, associé aux histoires que vous venez de lire, vous permettra, nous l'espérons, de comprendre les enjeux relevés par chaque skipper à bord de son bateau et d'analyser et de replacer dans leur contexte les faits de course, qu'ils surviennent à l'avant ou à l'arrière de la flotte.

L'écriture de ce livre a pris fin à l'été 2016. À cette date, trente skippers sont inscrits, mais tous ne sont pas encore qualifiés. Il est possible que certains d'entre eux ne puissent officiellement prendre le départ aux Sables-d'Olonne.

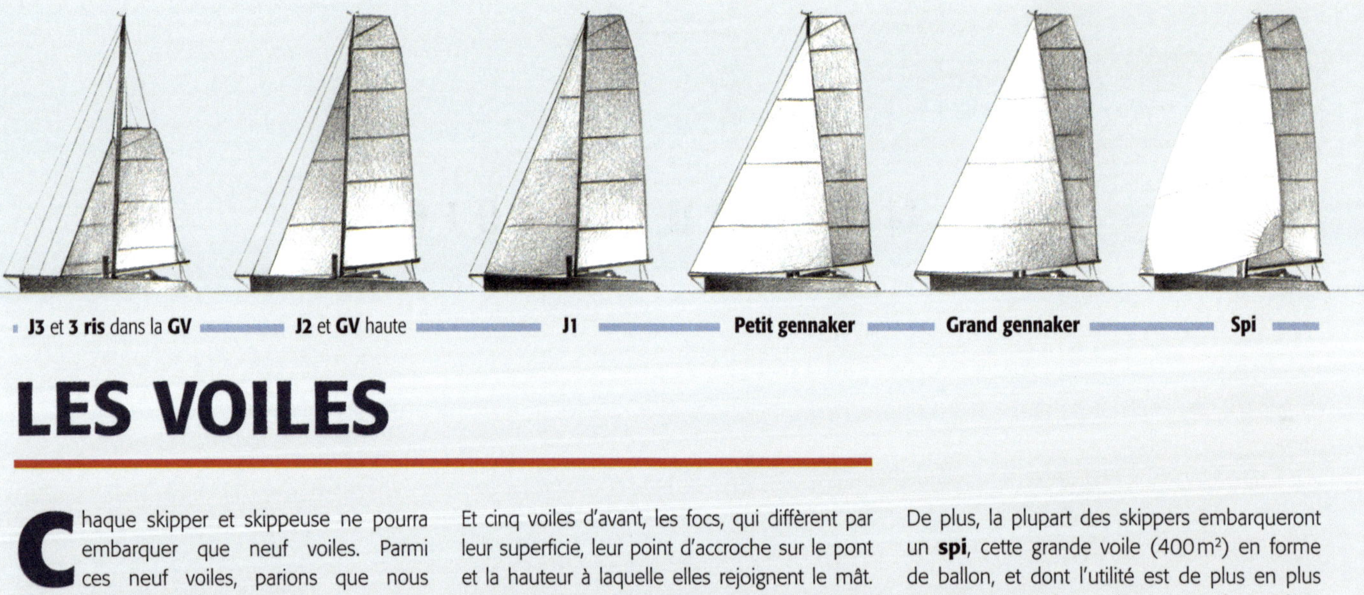

J3 et **3 ris** dans la **GV** — **J2** et **GV** haute — **J1** — **Petit gennaker** — **Grand gennaker** — **Spi**

LES VOILES

Chaque skipper et skippeuse ne pourra embarquer que neuf voiles. Parmi ces neuf voiles, parions que nous retrouverons sur tous les bateaux :

Une **grand-voile** (GV), la seule située à l'arrière du mât, d'environ 180 m² et dont on pourra réduire la superficie en prenant un, deux, ou trois ris. Dans les cas extrêmes, en tempête, on pourra complètement l'affaler et alors seule la corne de la voile (le haut de celle-ci) continuera à prendre le vent. Le **tourmentin**, une toute petite voile d'avant prévue seulement pour des conditions de tempête, ne sert, dans les faits, plus à grand-chose mais reste obligatoire à bord.

Et cinq voiles d'avant, les focs, qui diffèrent par leur superficie, leur point d'accroche sur le pont et la hauteur à laquelle elles rejoignent le mât. Les formes, plus ou moins creusées, ainsi que les tissus et les techniques de tissage ne cessent d'évoluer, au point que l'usure devient un facteur mineur dans le choix. Chaque voile aura une plage d'utilisation définie selon la force et l'angle du vent. Des noms différents désignent souvent des voiles très proches dont voici une liste, avec, en gras, un jeu "classique" : trinquette, **J3** (50 m²), ORC, **J2** (100 m²), **J1** (140 m²), solent, **petit gennaker** (200 m²), génois, code zéro, gennaker, reacher, **grand gennaker** (300 m²).

De plus, la plupart des skippers embarqueront un **spi**, cette grande voile (400 m²) en forme de ballon, et dont l'utilité est de plus en plus discutée, le grand gennaker pouvant le suppléer. Il reste donc une **neuvième voile**… et à son égard, motus et bouche cousue, chaque équipe a ses idées sur la question et l'on vous renverra aux pages 50 à 55.

Mais si l'on a droit à neuf voiles sur le Vendée Globe, celles-ci sont chères, de plus en plus chères et nombre de bateaux partiront avec un jeu de voiles moins étoffé, parfois même constitué de voiles d'occasion.

LES FOILS

Les bateaux sont équipés de deux dérives. Ces grandes "planches", parfois légèrement arrondies, sont des appendices qui traversent de haut en bas la coque plus ou moins au niveau du mât, et qui peuvent se plonger plus ou moins dans l'eau. Les dérives servent à contrer l'effet des forces voulant faire avancer le bateau en crabe. Le Vendée Globe 2016 voit arriver une évolution radicale de ces appendices : les foils. Ce sont ces mêmes "planches" mais cette fois fortement courbées, en forme de U, et qui donnent au bateau l'impression d'être moustachu. Elles sont situées peu ou prou aux mêmes endroits que les dérives classiques.

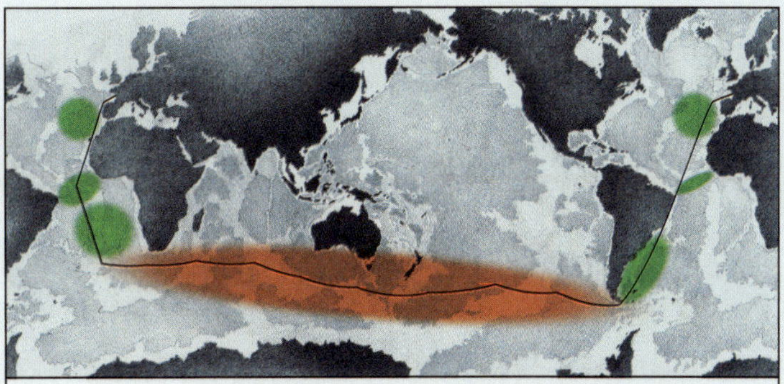

En vert, les zones où les probabilités de vent faible ou au près prédominent. Les bateaux à dérives traditionnelles devraient y être plus véloces. En rouge, les zones où ce sont majoritairement les vents forts et aux allures portantes que les skippers rencontreront. Les bateaux munis de foils y seront avantagés. Dans la zone des mers du Sud, en rouge, il faut garder en mémoire que, même aux vitesses maximales, aucun bateau ne devrait être en capacité de "sauter" d'une dépression à l'autre. Et toujours dans cette zone, il devrait survenir une à deux petites phases de transition, non représentées sur la carte, qui pourraient se révéler décisives.

Dérives traditionnelles (ici, dérive au vent relevée)

Foils

Les foils permettent d'augmenter la vitesse des bateaux par vent de travers à vent arrière, et par vent soutenu. En revanche, par rapport aux dérives traditionnelles, ils sont plus lents par petit temps et par vent de travers à vent dans le nez.
Si les premières versions de foils se sont avérées répondre à cette théorie, nous avons vu que les versions suivantes, v2 et v3 sur certains bateaux, ont permis de diminuer la perte de vitesse par vent faible et au près, faisant même jeu égal avec les dérives traditionnelles. Au portant et bon vent, le gain attendu de deux nœuds s'est avéré atteindre trois nœuds sur certaines phases !

Ces gains de vitesse sont obtenus grâce à une augmentation de la puissance créée par le navire. Celle-ci, générée par les foils, se répercute sur l'ensemble des éléments du bateau qu'il faut, par conséquent, renforcer et donc alourdir. Mais cette augmentation, qui a été sous-évaluée à la mise en place des foils, a valu démâtage, casse d'éléments structurels, début de naufrage… handicapant grandement la préparation de certains des nouveaux bateaux. Et l'on sait à quel point la qualité de la préparation a un impact sur la réussite lors d'un Vendée Globe. Au départ des Sables-d'Olonne, il semblerait toutefois que les bateaux soient prêts à affronter le tour du monde. Qu'en est-il alors des conditions de vie à bord de ces nouveaux bateaux?

Car effectivement, les "effets secondaires" pourraient bien être l'enjeu principal des foils. Le constat est unanime : ils induisent des comportements violents, notamment lors des décélérations, réclament une très bonne forme physique sur le long terme, et le bruit qu'ils génèrent, un sifflement permanent, ronge le mental. Les supporters des foils répliquent que "l'humain s'adapte à tout", certes. Mais qu'en est-il de la prise de décision, de l'analyse des fichiers météo, de la mise en place d'une stratégie dans des conditions nerveuses et physiques proches de l'épuisement?

Le match des foils n'est pas joué, et la casse en sera partie prenante. Et n'oublions pas que cette technologie est en cours de développement, chaque nouvelle version de foils en renforce les points forts et en réduit les points faibles.

Et qu'en est-il de la navigation? Les bateaux à dérives traditionnelles vont miser sur les phases de transition, caractérisées par un petit temps, tandis que les bateaux équipés de foils devront parier sur les phases stables par vents forts et portants. C'est une remise en cause profonde et passionnante de la stratégie de course au large, une recherche de polyvalence basée sur d'autres critères et nous vous invitons à relire les pages 22 à 25 au regard de cette nouvelle donne. Ajoutons que les gains des bateaux équipés de foils devront être importants, car les vitesses atteintes ne devraient toujours pas permettre de "sauter" d'une dépression à l'autre (page 46). La confrontation entre les foils et les dérives traditionnelles s'annonce exceptionnelle et à rebondissements. Espérons, pour notre plaisir de spectateur et de spectatrice, qu'elle se poursuive tout au long de la course.
Mais gardons en tête qu'aujourd'hui s'équiper de foils a un coût élevé, très élevé, et que seules les équipes les mieux loties peuvent se le permettre.

LES SKIPPERS
ENGAGÉS SUR LE VENDÉE GLOBE 2016

30 skippers sur la ligne de départ, 15 sur la ligne d'arrivée, c'est la dure et réaliste loi du Vendée Globe. Depuis la première édition en 1989, la course enregistre 50 % d'abandons pour des raisons multiples dont témoigne ce livre. Et plus la technologie se complexifie, plus l'humain se révèle l'enjeu majeur de la réussite ou non du tour du monde de chacun et chacune. Les skippers doivent être de plus en plus complets, physiquement, physiologiquement, émotionnellement, manuellement et intellectuellement.

LES PRÉTENDANTS AU PODIUM

Armel Le Cléac'h (39 ans) : Deux participations au Vendée Globe – 2008 et 2012 –, deux fois deuxième... Armel Le Cléac'h, à bord du bateau neuf le plus testé et fiabilisé de la flotte, est LE favori du Vendée Globe 2016. Le budget que lui alloue son sponsor peut être qualifié d'illimité. N'hésitant pas à optionner, n'aimant pas le jeu du "à-la-queuleuleu-à-celui-qui-cassera-le-premier", Armel devrait proposer suspense et stress aux spectateurs et spectatrices. Que du bon !

Vainqueur de ***The Transat*** *(2016) et de la* ***Solitaire du Figaro*** *(2003, 2010)*
VG *: 2008 [2ᵉ] 2012 [2ᵉ]*

Sébastien Josse (41 ans) : Il s'aligne avec un bateau neuf, un budget illimité et une énorme expérience de la navigation au long cours en équipage, ce qui signifie une concentration et des hautes vitesses permanentes. Il accumule un nombre impressionnant de milles, en course et en record, en monocoque et en multicoque. À la mise à l'eau, trop peu de confort semblait avoir été prévu au profit strict de la performance et, depuis, la radicalité de la machine semble avoir été revue. L'équilibre trouvé entre ces deux aspects devrait permettre à Sébastien Josse de naviguer aux avant-postes. Pour sa troisième participation au Vendée Globe, l'objectif est clairement affiché, la première place.

VG *: 2004 [5ᵉ] 2008 [ab.]*

Vincent Riou (44 ans) : Le couple que Vincent forme avec son bateau est sans nul doute le plus abouti de la flotte. La machine est optimisée et fiabilisée comme aucune autre et le marin semble n'avoir jamais autant maîtrisé son sujet... alors qu'il a déjà gagné le Vendée Globe en 2004 ! Il est le seul des quatre grands favoris à ne pas avoir un bateau équipé de foils. Il ne fait aucun doute que Vincent Riou sera l'un des skippers les plus observés de la flotte.

Vainqueur du ***Vendée Globe*** *(2004) et de la* ***Transat Jacques-Vabre*** *(2013, 2015)*
VG *: 2004 [1ᵉʳ] 2008 [3ᵉ voir p. 76 à 87] 2012 [ab.]*

Alex Thomson (42 ans) : Les spectateurs et spectatrices avertis, et plusieurs participants et participantes, désignent le parcours du navigateur lors de la dernière édition du Vendée Globe comme la plus belle performance de la course. Avec son bateau "d'ancienne" génération, il s'est hissé sur la troisième marche du podium. Alex Thomson fonce, semble physiquement résister aux plus hautes vitesses... et casse souvent son bateau. À bord du voilier neuf le plus typé pour la performance et le moins confortable, nul doute qu'il a toutes les cartes en main pour dépasser tout le monde. Mais cela lui permettra-t-il de vaincre son principal adversaire, lui-même ?

VG *: 2004 [ab.] 2008 [ab.] 2012 [3ᵉ]*

Jérémie Beyou (40 ans) : Il est le premier marin à avoir installé des foils sur un bateau d'ancienne génération. Ce choix lui a souri puisqu'il gagne, début 2016, la transatlantique de New York aux Sables-d'Olonne. Le lien avec son sponsor semble au beau fixe et sain, ce qui est une des clefs pour une bonne préparation... ce qui jusqu'ici avait toujours fait défaut au navigateur.

Vainqueur de la ***Solitaire du Figaro*** *(2005, 2011, 2014), de la* ***Transat Jacques-Vabre*** *(2011 avec Jean-Pierre Dick) et de la* ***New York-Les Sables***
VG *: 2008 [ab., voir p. 16 à 19] 2012 [ab.]*

Jean-Pierre Dick (50 ans) : Bateau neuf, participation aux trois dernières éditions du Vendée Globe, sponsors fidèles et consistants, tous les feux étaient au vert pour ce marin. Mais une casse structurelle du bateau est venue chambouler la préparation... Côté bonhomme, Jean-Pierre Dick est réputé entier dans son engagement physique, parfois trop ! Au risque de s'épuiser, de perdre sa lucidité, le marin engage. Et quand ça tient, il navigue extrêmement bien, commettant très peu d'erreurs. Ses nombreuses victoires en double le prouvent. Alors saura-t-il lever le pied et se ménager ?

Vainqueur de la ***Transat Jacques-Vabre*** *(2003 avec Nicolas Abiven, 2008 avec Loïck Peyron, 2011 avec Jérémie Beyou) et de la* ***Barcelona World Race*** *(2008 avec Damian Foxall, 2011 avec Loïck Peyron)*
VG *: 2004 [6ᵉ] 2008 [ab.] 2012 [4ᵉ]*

Yann Eliès (42 ans) : Deux fois détenteur du Trophée Jules-Verne, le record de vitesse du tour du monde en équipage, en 2002 et 2005. C'est pourtant sur le circuit Figaro que le marin excelle. Il remporte trois fois le trophée et compte le plus de victoires d'étape, à égalité avec Jean Le Cam. Il revient sur la course avec le bateau "le plus ancien parmi les prétendants au podium" mais optimisé de fond en comble.

Vainqueur de la ***Solitaire du Figaro*** *(2012, 2013, 2015)*
VG *: 2008 [ab.]*

LES OUTSIDERS

Morgan Lagravière (29 ans) : Première participation au Vendée Globe, il sera à bord d'un bateau neuf. L'ambition sportive est donc au rendez-vous, surtout lorsque l'on est coaché par **Roland Jourdain**. Sa manière de communiquer durant la transatlantique de New York aux Sables-d'Olonne dénote par rapport aux communications des autres skippers – en bien ! – Se révélera-t-il le skipper humainement le plus attachant, voire le plus drôle, du peloton de tête ?

Paul Meilhat (34 ans) : Première participation au Vendée Globe, il sera à bord du bateau vainqueur de la précédente édition, celui de François Gabart, et est coaché par **Michel Desjoyeaux**. Sa préparation a été chamboulée par un grave accident survenu en course en 2015, qui a obligé le skipper et la machine à consacrer du temps, et donc en perdre, pour se remettre sur pied.

DEUXIÈME DIVISION

Jean Le Cam (57 ans) : Le "Roi Jean" est une légende de la course au large. Il se présente sur la ligne de départ avec un temps récent de navigation et un budget bien en deçà de ce que l'on pourrait espérer pour un tel marin.
Il est l'exemple parfait qu'aujourd'hui, pour participer au Vendée Globe, il ne suffit pas d'être un excellent régatier, il faut aussi savoir se vendre, démarcher, courir les réunions… Il connaît parfaitement son bateau et, malgré sa préparation tronquée, pourrait tout de même se hisser dans le top 5.

*Vainqueur de la **Solitaire du Figaro** (1994, 1996, 1999), de la **Transat Jacques-Vabre** (2013 avec Vincent Riou) et de la **Barcelona World Race** (2015 avec Bernard Stamm)*
***VG** : 2004 [2e] 2008 [ab., voir p. 76 à 87] 2012 [5e]*

Thomas Ruyant, 35 ans, est le skipper qui, de par ses capacités de marin et son bateau, semble le plus apte à remporter cette division.

Kito de Pavant (55 ans, *VG 2008 [ab.] 2012 [ab.]*).

Arnaud Boissières (44 ans) : Les premiers jours et les descentes de l'Atlantique de ce marin, lent à l'allumage, ont souvent été en deçà de ce que l'on peut attendre sportivement de lui. Ses trajectoires dans le Grand Sud, aussi bien en 2008 qu'en 2012, prouvent qu'il est capable de sublimer sa machine, croquant à plusieurs reprises des bateaux de générations plus récentes. Espérons qu'il sera enfin reconnu autant pour ses capacités sportives que pour son bagout et son langage imagé qui, il faut bien le reconnaître, régalent nos oreilles.

VG : 2008 [7e] 2012 [8e]

Tanguy de Lamotte (38 ans) : Son premier Vendée Globe, en 2012, a prouvé qu'il savait boucler la boucle. Depuis, les modifications qu'il a apportées à son nouveau bateau et son parcours sur la Transat Jacques-Vabre 2015 – aux côtés de Samantha Davies – montrent que Tanguy joue de plus en plus la carte de l'ambition sportive et de la recherche de performance. Retenons qu'en 2012, son bateau, alors aux mains d'Arnaud Boissières, a fini le parcours en 91 jours et que Tanguy s'est donné pour objectif d'être, en 2016, sous la barre des 84 jours !

VG : 2012 [10e]

TROISIÈME DIVISION

La division se justifie généralement par la génération trop ancienne du bateau.

Kojiro Shiraishi (49 ans) : Il est le marin apparu le plus tardivement sur les radars du Vendée Globe 2016. Apparition soudaine, il annonce pourtant s'aligner avec un bateau de belle facture et s'engage dans la transatlantique de New York aux Sables-d'Olonne où ses choix de trajectoires se révèlent extrêmement plaisants à suivre et à analyser. Son temps de préparation et notre méconnaissance à son égard – que nous avouons bien volontiers – nous le font placer en troisième division mais il y a fort à parier qu'on le retrouve plutôt en deuxième.

Romain Attanasio (39 ans) : Il n'a pu acheter l'ancien bateau de Tanguy de Lamotte qu'extrêmement tardivement, ne bénéficie que d'un petit budget et d'un temps restreint de prise en main et de fiabilisation sur l'eau. Mais lorsque la possibilité d'un Vendée Globe est là, le régatier confirmé qu'il est ne peut que répondre à l'appel du tour du monde en solitaire, sans escale et sans assistance !
Il est secondé dans sa préparation par **Samantha Davies**.

Et **Bertrand de Broc** (55 ans, excellent régatier, *VG 1992 [ab.] 1996 [ab.] 2012 [9e]*), **Louis Burton** (31 ans, *VG 2012 [ab.]*), **Éric Bellion** (40 ans) et **Fabrice Amedeo** (38 ans).

Nous n'avons pas classé les skippers ci-dessous, car nous n'avons pas assez de renseignements pertinents à leur propos.

Conrad Colman (32 ans), **Didac Costa** (35 ans), **Sébastien Destremau** (51 ans, excellent régatier), **Stéphane Le Diraison** (40 ans), **Alan Roura** (23 ans), **Jean-François Pellet** (46 ans), **Nandor Fa** (63 ans, *VG 1992 [5e] 1996 [ab.]*), **Rich Wilson** (66 ans, *VG 2008 [9e]*), **Enda O'Coineen** (60 ans), **Pieter Heerema** (65 ans) s'est payé sur ses fonds propres un bateau de dernière génération équipé de foils… et navigue selon son âge et avec un palmarès en solo en course au large relativement vierge, l'argent ne fait pas tout.

Si, parmi les acteurs de ce livre, seul **François Gabart** n'apparaît pas ici, c'est qu'il se dédie à la navigation en Ultim, trimaran de 30 mètres prévu pour le solitaire et… les tours du monde. Plusieurs figures du Vendée Globe devraient bientôt le rejoindre dans cette aventure.

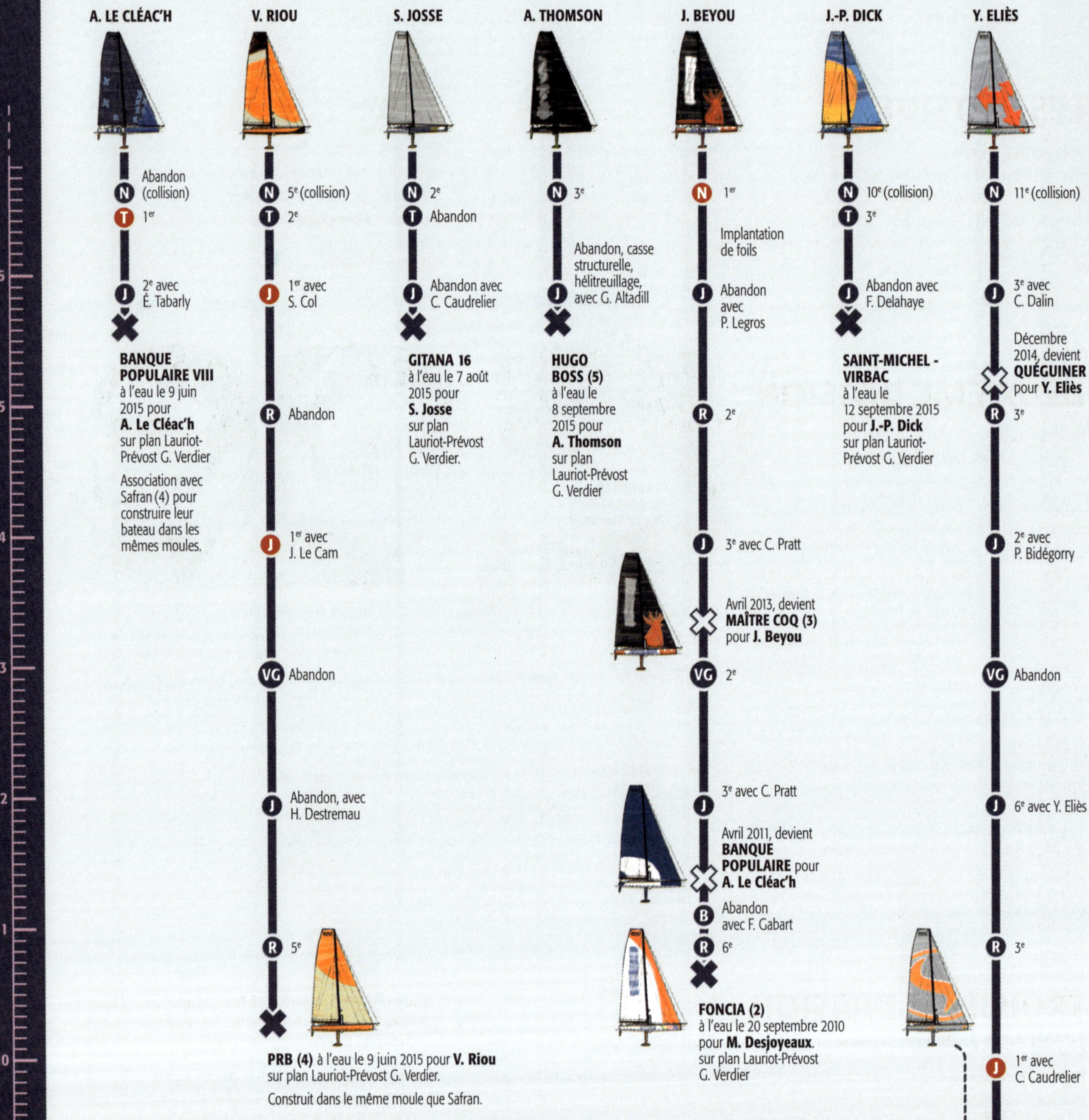

LES BATEAUX 2016

PAR L'ŒIL DE LA RÉGATE

- **J** **Transat Jacques-Vabre :** Transatlantique France-Brésil, en double.
- **T** **The Transat :** Transatlantique Angleterre-États-Unis (contre les vents), en solitaire.
- **B** **Barcelona World Race :** Tour du monde à partir de Barcelone (Espagne), en double, escales autorisées.
- **N** **New York-Vendée :** Transatlantique en solitaire.
- **R** **Route du Rhum :** Transatlantique France-Guadeloupe, en solitaire.
- **Bo** **Boc Challenge**, puis Around Alone, puis Velux 5 Oceans : Tour du monde avec escales, en solitaire.
- **VG** **Vendée Globe :** Tour du monde à partir des Sables-d'Olonne, en solitaire, sans escale.

La compétition reine de la classe Imoca est sans conteste le Vendée Globe. Toutes les autres courses du circuit sont courues pour leur intérêt sportif et comme entraînement au tour du monde en solitaire. Nous n'avons référencé que six autres courses, les principales, bien sûr de nombreuses autres existent. Si l'on veut imaginer ce que sera le Vendée Globe, il faut se méfier du classement de ces courses et notamment de l'abandon. La manière de naviguer est souvent plus révélatrice du niveau réel du bateau et du skipper. Enfin, on peut estimer qu'un bateau participant à ces courses est bien entretenu et a sans cesse reçu des modifications en quête de performances.

Un grand merci à www.histoiredeshalfs.com pour tout son travail. Les chiffres entre parenthèses sont donnés pour distinguer deux bateaux portant le même nom, ils n'ont rien d'officiel. Les couleurs des bateaux sont des "approximations artistiques" et certaines équipes n'ont pas encore dévoilé leurs couleurs pour le Vendée Globe 2016.

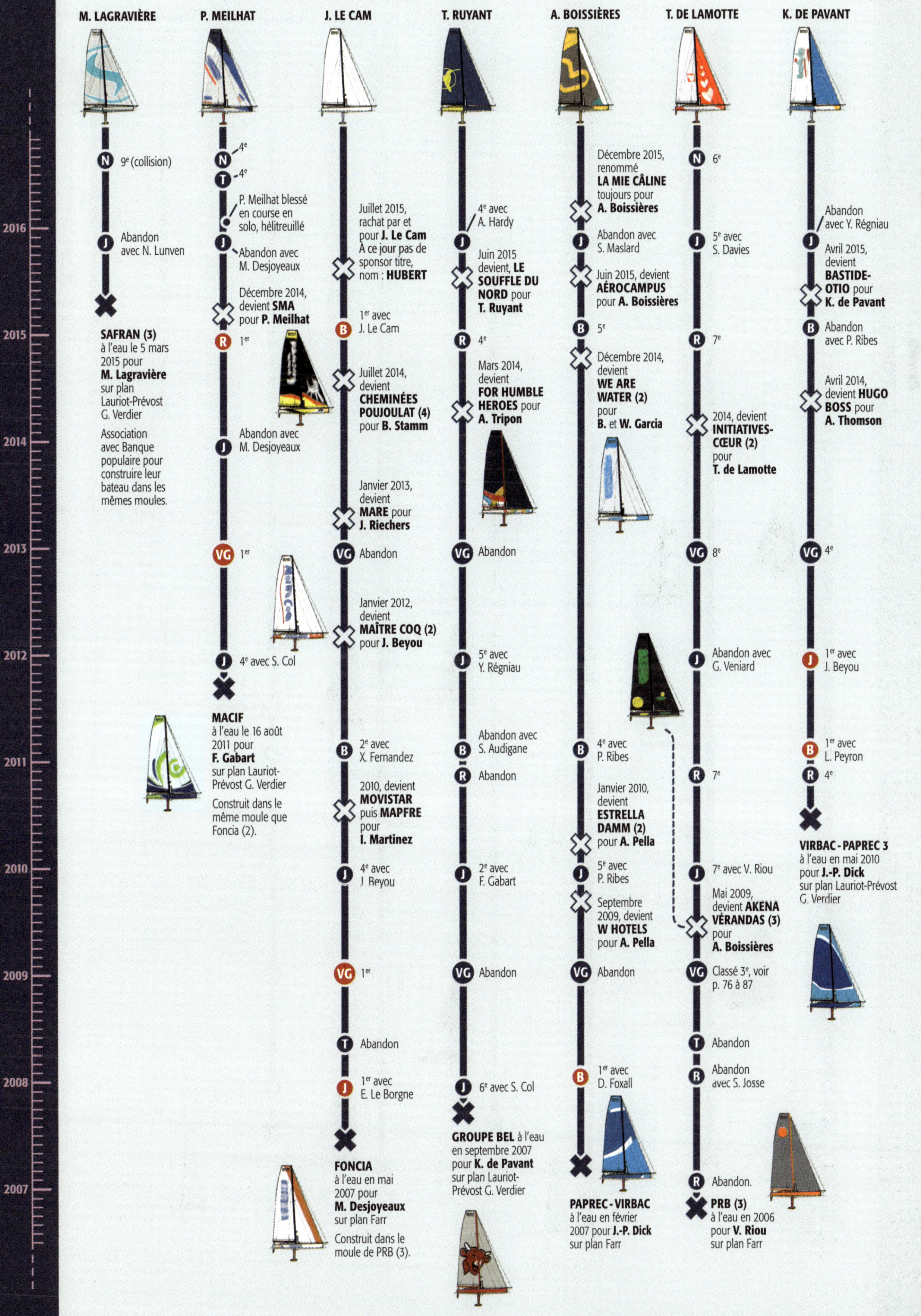

2016
2015
2014
2013
2012
2011
2010
2009
2008
2007
M. LAGRAVIÈRE
N 9e (collision)
J Abandon avec N. Lunven
SAFRAN (3) à l'eau le 5 mars 2015 pour M. Lagravière sur plan Lauriot-Prévost G. Verdier
Association avec Banque populaire pour construire leur bateau dans les mêmes moules.
P. MEILHAT
N 4e
T 4e
P. Meilhat blessé en course en solo, hélitreuillé
J Abandon avec M. Desjoyeaux
Décembre 2014, devient SMA pour P. Meilhat
R 1er
J Abandon avec M. Desjoyeaux
VG 1er
J 4e avec S. Col
MACIF à l'eau le 16 août 2011 pour F. Gabart sur plan Lauriot-Prévost G. Verdier
Construit dans le même moule que Foncia (2).
J. LE CAM
Juillet 2015, rachat par et pour J. Le Cam À ce jour pas de sponsor titre, nom : HUBERT
B 1er avec J. Le Cam
Juillet 2014, devient CHEMINÉES POUJOULAT (4) pour B. Stamm
Janvier 2013, devient MARE pour J. Riechers
VG Abandon
Janvier 2012, devient MAÎTRE COQ (2) pour J. Beyou
B 2e avec X. Fernandez
2010, devient MOVISTAR puis MAPFRE pour I. Martinez
J 4e avec J. Beyou
VG 1er
T Abandon
J 1er avec E. Le Borgne
FONCIA à l'eau en mai 2007 pour M. Desjoyeaux sur plan Farr
Construit dans le moule de PRB (3).
T. RUYANT
J 4e avec A. Hardy
Juin 2015 devient, LE SOUFFLE DU NORD pour T. Ruyant
R 4e
Mars 2014, devient FOR HUMBLE HEROES pour A. Tripon
VG Abandon
J 5e avec Y. Régniau
B Abandon avec S. Audigane
R Abandon
J 2e avec F. Gabart
VG Abandon
J 6e avec S. Col
GROUPE BEL à l'eau en septembre 2007 pour K. de Pavant sur plan Lauriot-Prévost G. Verdier
A. BOISSIÈRES
Décembre 2015, renommé LA MIE CÂLINE toujours pour A. Boissières
J Abandon avec S. Maslard
Juin 2015, devient AÉROCAMPUS pour A. Boissières
B 5e
Décembre 2014, devient WE ARE WATER (2) pour B. et W. Garcia
B 4e avec P. Ribes
Janvier 2010, devient ESTRELLA DAMM (2) pour A. Pella
J 5e avec P. Ribes
Septembre 2009, devient W HOTELS pour A. Pella
VG Abandon
B 1er avec D. Foxall
PAPREC-VIRBAC à l'eau en février 2007 pour J.-P. Dick sur plan Farr
T. DE LAMOTTE
N 6e
J 5e avec S. Davies
R 7e
2014, devient INITIATIVES-CŒUR (2) pour T. de Lamotte
VG 8e
J Abandon avec G. Veniard
R 7e
J 7e avec V. Riou
Mai 2009, devient AKENA VÉRANDAS (3) pour A. Boissières
VG Classé 3e, voir p. 76 à 87
T Abandon
B Abandon avec S. Josse
R Abandon.
PRB (3) à l'eau en 2006 pour V. Riou sur plan Farr
K. DE PAVANT
J Abandon avec Y. Régniau
Avril 2015, devient BASTIDE-OTIO pour K. de Pavant
B Abandon avec P. Ribes
Avril 2014, devient HUGO BOSS pour A. Thomson
VG 4e
J 1er avec J. Beyou
B 1er avec L. Peyron
R 4e
VIRBAC-PAPREC 3 à l'eau en mai 2010 pour J.-P. Dick sur plan Lauriot-Prévost G. Verdier

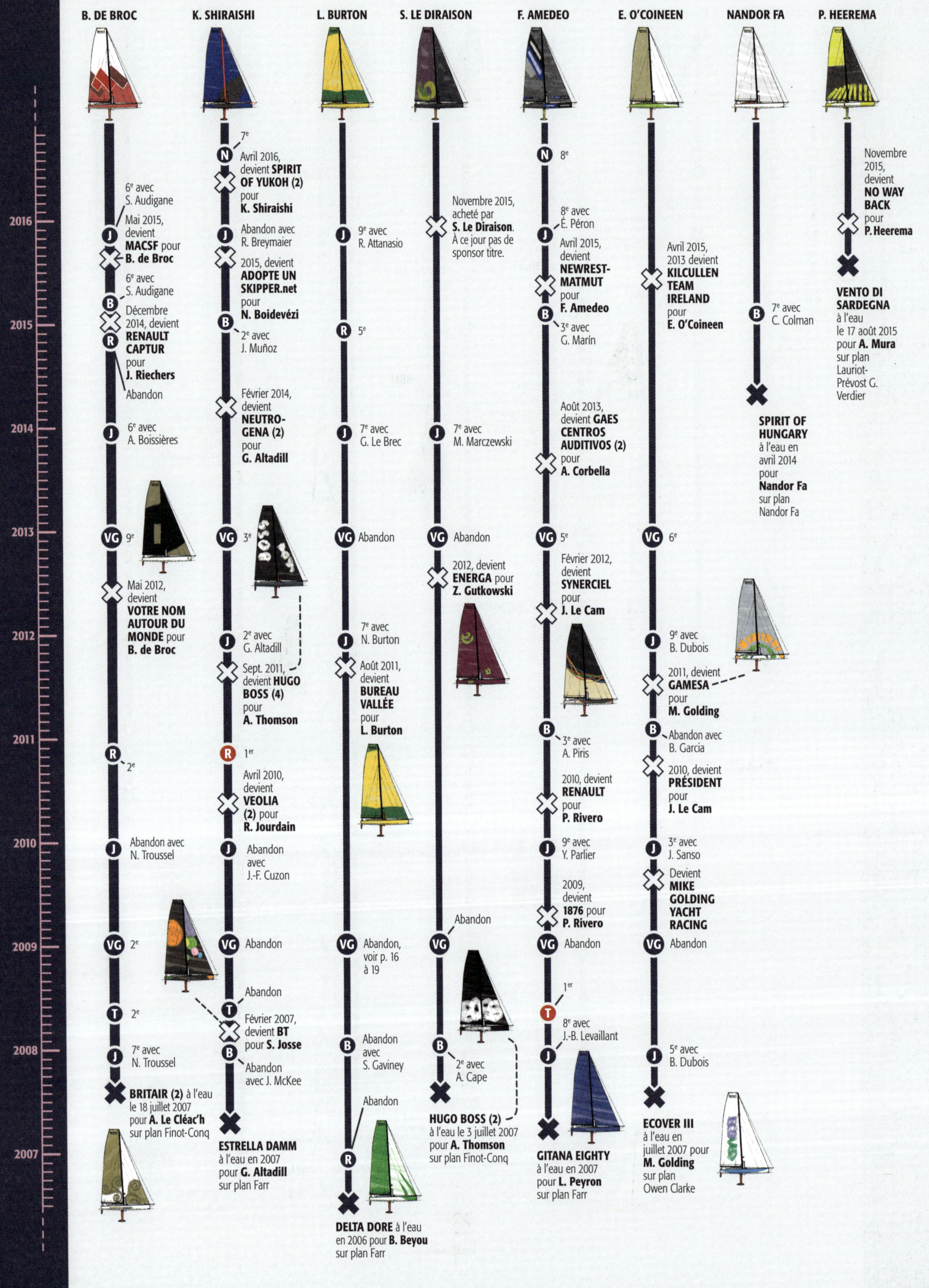
2016
2015
2014
2013
2012
2011
2010
2009
2008
2007
B. DE BROC
6e avec S. Audigane
Mai 2015, devient MACSF pour B. de Broc
J
6e avec S. Audigane
B
Décembre 2014, devient RENAULT CAPTUR pour J. Riechers
R
Abandon
J 6e avec A. Boissières
VG 9e
Mai 2012, devient VOTRE NOM AUTOUR DU MONDE pour B. de Broc
R 2e
J Abandon avec N. Troussel
VG 2e
T 2e
J 7e avec N. Troussel
BRITAIR (2) à l'eau le 18 juillet 2007 pour A. Le Cléac'h sur plan Finot-Conq
K. SHIRAISHI
N 7e
Avril 2016, devient SPIRIT OF YUKOH (2) pour K. Shiraishi
J Abandon avec R. Breymaier
2015, devient ADOPTE UN SKIPPER.net pour N. Boidevézi
B 2e avec J. Muñoz
Février 2014, devient NEUTRO-GENA (2) pour G. Altadill
VG 3e
J 2e avec G. Altadill
Sept. 2011, devient HUGO BOSS (4) pour A. Thomson
R 1er
Avril 2010, devient VEOLIA (2) pour R. Jourdain
J Abandon avec J.-F. Cuzon
VG Abandon
T Abandon
Février 2007, devient BT pour S. Josse
B Abandon avec J. McKee
ESTRELLA DAMM à l'eau en 2007 pour G. Altadill sur plan Farr
L. BURTON
J 9e avec R. Attanasio
R 5e
J 7e avec G. Le Brec
VG Abandon
J 7e avec N. Burton
Août 2011, devient BUREAU VALLÉE pour L. Burton
VG Abandon, voir p. 16 à 19
B Abandon avec S. Gaviney
R Abandon
DELTA DORE à l'eau en 2006 pour B. Beyou sur plan Farr
S. LE DIRAISON
Novembre 2015, acheté par S. Le Diraison. À ce jour pas de sponsor titre.
J 7e avec M. Marczewski
VG Abandon
2012, devient ENERGA pour Z. Gutkowski
VG Abandon
B 2e avec A. Cape
HUGO BOSS (2) à l'eau le 3 juillet 2007 pour A. Thomson sur plan Finot-Conq
F. AMEDEO
N 8e
J 8e avec É. Péron
Avril 2015, devient NEWREST-MATMUT pour F. Amedeo
B 3e avec G. Marín
Août 2013, devient GAES CENTROS AUDITIVOS (2) pour A. Corbella
VG 5e
Février 2012, devient SYNERCIEL pour J. Le Cam
B 3e avec A. Piris
2010, devient RENAULT pour P. Rivero
J 9e avec Y. Parlier
2009, devient 1876 pour P. Rivero
VG Abandon
T 1er
J 8e avec J.-B. Levaillant
GITANA EIGHTY à l'eau en 2007 pour L. Peyron sur plan Farr
E. O'COINEEN
Avril 2015, 2013 devient KILCULLEN TEAM IRELAND pour E. O'Coineen
VG 6e
J 9e avec B. Dubois
2011, devient GAMESA pour M. Golding
B Abandon avec B. Garcia
2010, devient PRÉSIDENT pour J. Le Cam
J 3e avec J. Sanso
Devient MIKE GOLDING YACHT RACING
VG Abandon
J 5e avec B. Dubois
ECOVER III à l'eau en juillet 2007 pour M. Golding sur plan Owen Clarke
NANDOR FA
B 7e avec C. Colman
SPIRIT OF HUNGARY à l'eau en avril 2014 pour Nandor Fa sur plan Nandor Fa
P. HEEREMA
Novembre 2015, devient NO WAY BACK pour P. Heerema
VENTO DI SARDEGNA à l'eau le 17 août 2015 pour A. Mura sur plan Lauriot-Prévost G. Verdier

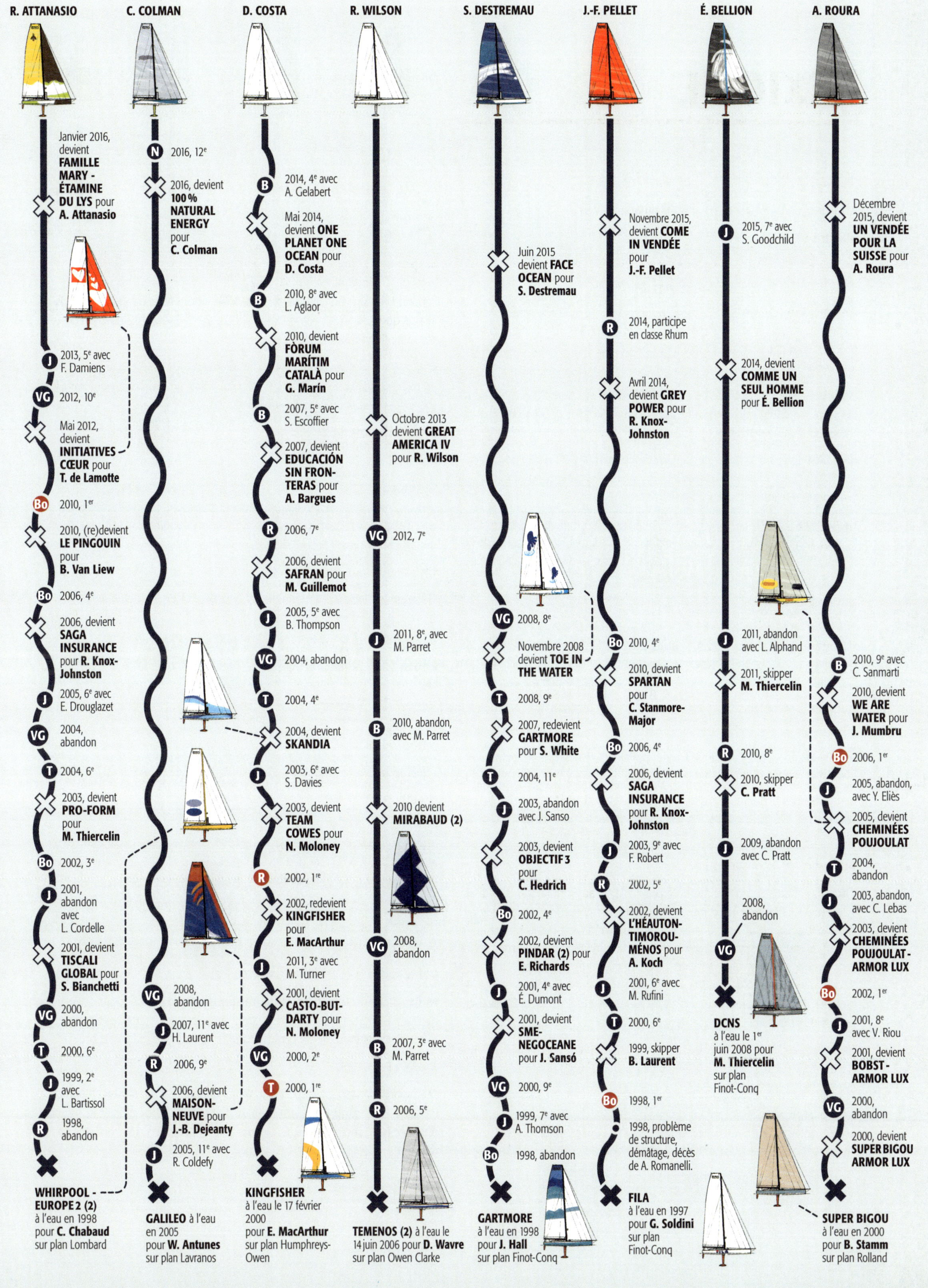
R. ATTANASIO
Janvier 2016, devient FAMILLE MARY - ÉTAMINE DU LYS pour A. Attanasio
J 2013, 5e avec F. Damiens
VG 2012, 10e
Mai 2012, devient INITIATIVES CŒUR pour T. de Lamotte
Bo 2010, 1er
2010, (re)devient LE PINGOUIN pour B. Van Liew
Bo 2006, 4e
2006, devient SAGA INSURANCE pour R. Knox-Johnston
J 2005, 6e avec E. Drouglazet
VG 2004, abandon
T 2004, 6e
2003, devient PRO-FORM pour M. Thiercelin
Bo 2002, 3e
J 2001, abandon avec L. Cordelle
2001, devient TISCALI GLOBAL pour S. Bianchetti
VG 2000, abandon
T 2000, 6e
J 1999, 2e avec L. Bartissol
R 1998, abandon
WHIRPOOL - EUROPE 2 (2) à l'eau en 1998 pour C. Chabaud sur plan Lombard
C. COLMAN
N 2016, 12e
2016, devient 100 % NATURAL ENERGY pour C. Colman
VG 2008, abandon
J 2007, 11e avec H. Laurent
R 2006, 9e
2006, devient MAISON-NEUVE pour J.-B. Dejeanty
J 2005, 11e avec R. Coldefy
GALILEO à l'eau en 2005 pour W. Antunes sur plan Lavranos
D. COSTA
B 2014, 4e avec A. Gelabert
Mai 2014, devient ONE PLANET ONE OCEAN pour D. Costa
B 2010, 8e avec L. Aglaor
2010, devient FÒRUM MARÍTIM CATALÀ pour G. Marín
B 2007, 5e avec S. Escoffier
2007, devient EDUCACIÓN SIN FRON-TERAS pour A. Bargues
R 2006, 7e
2006, devient SAFRAN pour M. Guillemot
J 2005, 5e avec B. Thompson
VG 2004, abandon
T 2004, 4e
2004, devient SKANDIA
J 2003, 6e avec S. Davies
2003, devient TEAM COWES pour N. Moloney
R 2002, 1re
2002, redevient KINGFISHER pour E. MacArthur
J 2011, 3e avec M. Turner
2001, devient CASTO-BUT-DARTY pour N. Moloney
VG 2000, 2e
T 2000, 1re
KINGFISHER à l'eau le 17 février 2000 pour E. MacArthur sur plan Humphreys-Owen
R. WILSON
Octobre 2013 devient GREAT AMERICA IV pour R. Wilson
VG 2012, 7e
J 2011, 8e, avec M. Parret
B 2010, abandon, avec M. Parret
2010 devient MIRABAUD (2)
VG 2008, abandon
B 2007, 3e avec M. Parret
R 2006, 5e
TEMENOS (2) à l'eau le 14 juin 2006 pour D. Wavre sur plan Owen Clarke
S. DESTREMAU
Juin 2015 devient FACE OCEAN pour S. Destremau
VG 2008, 8e
Novembre 2008 devient TOE IN THE WATER
T 2008, 9e
2007, redevient GARTMORE pour S. White
T 2004, 11e
J 2003, abandon avec J. Sanso
2003, devient OBJECTIF 3 pour C. Hedrich
Bo 2002, 4e
2002, devient PINDAR (2) pour E. Richards
J 2001, 4e avec É. Dumont
2001, devient SME-NEGOCEANE pour J. Sansó
VG 2000, 9e
J 1999, 7e avec A. Thomson
Bo 1998, abandon
GARTMORE à l'eau en 1998 pour J. Hall sur plan Finot-Conq
J.-F. PELLET
Novembre 2015, devient COME IN VENDÉE pour J.-F. Pellet
R 2014, participe en classe Rhum
Avril 2014, devient GREY POWER pour R. Knox-Johnston
Bo 2010, 4e
2010, devient SPARTAN pour C. Stanmore-Major
Bo 2006, 4e
2006, devient SAGA INSURANCE pour R. Knox-Johnston
J 2003, 9e avec F. Robert
R 2002, 5e
2002, devient L'HÉAUTON-TIMOROU-MÉNOS pour A. Koch
J 2001, 6e avec M. Rufini
T 2000, 6e
1999, skipper B. Laurent
Bo 1998, 1er
1998, problème de structure, démâtage, décès de A. Romanelli.
FILA à l'eau en 1997 pour G. Soldini sur plan Finot-Conq
É. BELLION
J 2015, 7e avec S. Goodchild
2014, devient COMME UN SEUL HOMME pour É. Bellion
J 2011, abandon avec L. Alphand
2011, skipper M. Thiercelin
R 2010, 8e
2010, skipper C. Pratt
J 2009, abandon avec C. Pratt
VG 2008, abandon
DCNS à l'eau le 1er juin 2008 pour M. Thiercelin sur plan Finot-Conq
A. ROURA
Décembre 2015, devient UN VENDÉE POUR LA SUISSE pour A. Roura
B 2010, 9e avec C. Sanmarti
2010, devient WE ARE WATER pour J. Mumbru
Bo 2006, 1er
J 2005, abandon, avec Y. Eliès
2005, devient CHEMINÉES POUJOULAT
T 2004, abandon
J 2003, abandon, avec C. Lebas
2003, devient CHEMINÉES POUJOULAT - ARMOR LUX
Bo 2002, 1er
J 2001, 8e avec V. Riou
2001, devient BOBST - ARMOR LUX
VG 2000, abandon
2000, devient SUPER BIGOU ARMOR LUX
SUPER BIGOU à l'eau en 2000 pour B. Stamm sur plan Rolland

LEXIQUE

Ce lexique regroupe la plupart des mots techniques rencontrés dans ce livre. Il n'est pas exhaustif.

Abattée (partir à l'abattée) : Voir "tas (partir au tas)".

Abattre : S'écarter du vent.

Affaler : Descendre une voile, pour réduire sa superficie, la rendre complètement inopérante ou la remplacer par une autre.

Anticyclone : Système météo de hautes pressions se traduisant généralement par des vents calmes (pétole et petits airs), du soleil et de la chaleur (barbecues). Un anticyclone, comme une dépression, a généralement une forme de patate.

Ballasts : Réservoirs d'eau de mer lestant le bateau et répartis à différents endroits du bateau. Ils permettent de corriger la gîte, bâbord/tribord, ou l'assiette, proue/poupe.

Barres de flèche : Barres perpendiculaires au mât qui permettent d'écarter les haubans. Elles viennent toujours par deux symétriquement et on en retrouve à plusieurs hauteurs, les étages, du mât.

Bastaques : Ayant plus ou moins la même utilité que les haubans, elles vont de l'arrière du bateau à plusieurs points le long du mât. Elles rigidifient le mât dans l'axe du bateau. On tend celle au vent, tandis qu'on relâche celle sous le vent. Il y en a une de chaque côté.

Bord (rester sur le même bord) : Le bord est un des deux côtés du bateau, le bord bâbord et le bord tribord. On reste sur le même bord tant que le vent arrive du même côté, en oscillant de vent de face à vent arrière, et qu'on ne souhaite pas changer de direction. En pratique, cela signifie que l'on reste gîté du même côté tant qu'on ne change pas de bord.

Border : Tendre une voile, c'est-à-dire tirer sur l'écoute, généralement à l'aide des winchs ou du moulin à café. On dit que l'on "reprend de l'écoute".

Bout : Un bout – se prononce [but] – désigne tout type de cordage, de ficelle, de corde, voire, pourquoi pas, de lacet.

Bout-dehors : Excroissance surplombant l'eau et prolongeant le bateau vers l'avant. Elle permet notamment d'augmenter la capacité de voilure. On ne le voit que trop bien page 41.

Budget : Voir "sponsor".

Cap (direction) : Le 0° pointe au Nord, le 180° au Sud, le cap est l'angle que l'on tient pour aller dans la direction souhaitée. On navigue généralement avec pour but de suivre une route définie. Mais on peut aussi parler de cap par rapport au vent. Cela signifie alors que l'on s'intéresse à l'angle que le bateau forme avec l'axe d'où vient le vent. Naviguer selon le cap au vent permet de tenir une vitesse constante. Bien sûr, ce cap ne doit pas être confondu avec les caps géographiques, Bonne-Espérance, Leeuwin, Horn, etc.

Choquer : Détendre une voile, c'est-à-dire laisser filer l'écoute. Pour contrôler la vitesse, on peut se servir des winchs ou du moulin à café. On dit que l'on "lâche de l'écoute".

Dépression : Système météo de basses pressions se traduisant par des vents soutenus à l'inverse de l'anticyclone. Curieusement, ce serait plutôt ce dernier qui aurait pour effet de faire tomber le skipper en dépression.

Dérive : Lorsque le vent n'arrive pas strictement de l'arrière, il exerce une force dans l'axe de navigation et va donc créer une force de dérive sur le bateau. Le courant marin va avoir le même effet. On plonge alors des pales dans l'eau pour contrer ces forces et ne pas avancer en crabe. Ces pales s'appellent des dérives et sur les Imoca – voir page 119 le cas particulier des foils –, elles sont au nombre de deux, situées plus ou moins au niveau du mât. On peut les relever ou les immerger en fonction de l'effet souhaité.

Écoute : Bout assigné au contrôle d'une voile que l'on borde si l'on veut tendre la voile, ou que l'on choque si l'on veut la creuser.

Empanner : Changer de bord en passant par le vent arrière. Souvent jugé plus périlleux que le virement de bord en raison du choc subi par l'ensemble du gréement et du mât, mais permettant de perdre moins de temps que lors d'un virement – le fait de changer de bord mais en passant par vent debout cette fois.

Étai : Ayant plus ou moins la même utilité que les haubans, il va de l'avant du bateau au sommet du mât. On utilise également l'étai pour fixer tout son long une voile d'avant (voir page 118).

Étrave : L'avant du bateau.

Foc : Voir page 118.

Gréement : C'est l'ensemble de ce qui permet à un bateau d'avancer avec le vent, mât, bouts, voiles, etc. Le gréement est dit "de fortune" s'il est réalisé avec des bouts de bouts (voir définition), dans le cas d'un dématage par exemple.

GV : Grand-voile, voir page 118.

Haubans : Câbles arrimant le mât au bateau. Les haubans sont situés des deux côtés du mât, soit accrochés directement à la coque avec des barres de flèches pour les écarter, soit aux extrémités des outriggers.

Imoca : Les bateaux participant au Vendée Globe relèvent de l'Imoca, une classe "open". Aucun bateau n'est identique, chaque skipper peut faire construire et évoluer sa machine selon sa philosophie. C'est donc une classe où recherche et développement vont bon train, une classe où l'argent est un facteur déterminant. Pour des raisons de sécurité et d'équité sportive, l'Imoca édicte tout de même un grand nombre de règles définissant un cadre de jeu (voir page 14). L'Imoca est gérée et dirigée par les skippers et skippeuses s'inscrivant à la classe.

Lashing : C'est l'amarrage entre eux de deux éléments, par le truchement d'un petit bout très solide que l'on installe en une multitude d'allers-retours. Lorsque l'on dit que le "lashing pète", c'est que les deux éléments qu'il tenait ne sont plus solidaires (voir page 100).

Lofer : C'est le fait de se rapprocher du vent. Plus on lofe, plus on va s'approcher du vent de face. Lofer permet, en plus de tenir le cap que l'on s'est choisi, de réduire sa vitesse.

Lof (partir au lof) : Voir "tas (partir au tas)".

Mille, ou **mille marin** ou **mille nautique :** Unité de longueur correspondant à 1 852,30 mètres. En mer, c'est par cette unité que sont exprimées toutes les distances. À ne pas confondre avec le mile anglo-saxon.

Molle : Faible vent.

Monotypie : Une course courue en monotypie signifie que tous les bateaux sont strictement identiques. C'est l'inverse des courses relevant de "classes open" telles que l'Imoca (voir définition). Ces notions apparaissent en pages 14 et 15.

Nœud : Unité de vitesse correspondant à 1 mille à l'heure. Pour se faire une idée rapide, en kilomètres par heure, des vitesses exprimées en nœuds, on peut multiplier par deux et "enlever un peu". Une vitesse de 30 nœuds correspond à environ 55 km/h, 10 nœuds à 18 km/h.

Outriggers : Grandes "barres" sortant de chaque côté du bateau au niveau du mât. Ils ont la même fonction que les barres de flèches, mais ne nécessitent "qu'un étage" au niveau du pont.

Pétole : Pas de vent. Pas même un pet.

Polaires : Vitesses à atteindre en fonction des conditions de vent et de mer. Elles sont établies et mises à jour au cours de chaque navigation. Le but est de naviguer à 100 % de ses polaires, voire plus.

Pot-au-Noir : Aussi nommé "zone de convergence intertropicale". C'est une bande géographique se situant aux alentours de l'équateur. Elle se caractérise par une absence de vent.

Quille : Tige immergée prolongée d'un bulbe, lestant le bateau et permettant de maintenir l'embarcation dans le bon sens. Avec une quille pouvant basculer latéralement, on peut maintenir plus longtemps une gîte faible.

Ris : Système permettant de diminuer la surface de la grand-voile. Généralement, plus le vent se lève, plus on prend des ris.

Routage : Fait de définir la route, qui semble optimale, pour aller d'un point à un autre. Le routage prend en compte la météo, les courants, l'état de la mer et les différentes caractéristiques du bateau. Sur le Vendée Globe et plus généralement sur les courses régies par la classe Imoca, le skipper doit faire seul ses routages et ne peut être aidé par des personnes à terre. Il interprète les routages proposés par l'ordinateur selon la fiabilité donnée aux prévisions météo, son état de fatigue, la trajectoire des autres concurrents (voir pages 22 à 25 et 68 à 73) et sa vision stratégique à plus long terme que ne le permettent les informations météo (voir pages 56 à 59).

Safran : C'est la pale qui se trouve à l'arrière du bateau et qui permet de diriger celui-ci. Il y en a un de chaque côté sur les gros bateaux et ceux de course, généralement un seul, situé au milieu, sur les bateaux de plaisance. À ne pas confondre avec le nom d'un sponsor d'une des équipes du Vendée Globe.

Spare : On dit "du matériel de spare" ou "du spare". Il s'agit du matériel de rechange.

Sponsor : Voir "budget".

Surf (partir au surf) : Lorsque bateau et vague vont dans la même direction à grande vitesse, le bateau accélère d'un coup, s'arrachant de la retenue générée par l'eau.

Tas (partir au tas) : La marche normale d'un bateau est la coque au-dessus de l'eau, le mât et les voiles au-dessus de la coque, le tout plus ou moins penché. Il arrive cependant que cette marche normale soit mise en pétard, on parle alors souvent de "départ au tas". Il ne faut toutefois pas confondre un départ au lof, lorsque le bateau se couche sur l'eau du côté de la gîte, et un départ à l'abattée lorsque le bateau se couche sur l'eau, brutalement, de l'autre côté que la gîte. Dans le premier cas, l'effet est bénin (voir page 49), dans le second, la bascule coûte au moins quelques lattes cassées, si ce n'est plus (voir pages 26 à 31).

INDEX DES CITATIONS
PAR MARINS

INDEX DES CITATIONS
PAR PAGES

À Ann, pour son anniversaire.

LES AUTEURS REMERCIENT ET SALUENT : Didier Ravon, Denis Horeau, Yann, Myriam, Elliot et Paul Rochas, Gisèle Pape, Philippe Ostermann et François Le Bescond, Arnaud Boissières, Michel Desjoyeaux, Tanguy de Lamotte, Jean Le Cam, Yann Eliès, Jérémie Beyou, Roland Jourdain, Armel Le Cléac'h, François Gabart, Samantha Davies, David Brabis, Stéphanie Ruchaud, Christophe Boisset, Guillaume Le Fur, Philippe Ravon, Stéphana Chassin, Frédéric Augendre, Pierre-Marie Bourguinat, Laurence Caraes, Charline Hamonic, Fabienne Morin, Antoine Robin.

www.vendeeglobe.org
www.dargaud.com

Certifié PEFC
Ce produit est issu de forêts gérées durablement et de sources recyclées et contrôlées.
PEFC 10-31-1800
pefc-france.org

2016 PREMIÈRE ÉDITION

Dépôt légal : octobre 2016 – ISBN 978-2205-07563-2
Imprimé et relié en France par PPO Graphic, 91120 Palaiseau.